The Journey of A Rainbow . . .

The Journey of A Rainbow . . .

My Poetic Journal Mind Views

Minerva A. Garcia,
MS, MLS, MT (ASCP)

Print information available on the last page.

Rev. date: 03/26/2019

To order additional copies of this book, contact:
Xlibris
1-888-795-4274
www.Xlibris.com
Orders@Xlibris.com
536701

Contents

Dedication

These collections of poems are dedicated to the people who have come into my life and made an enormous impression and footprints onto my life for the better, because it made me aim to be who I am for the very best.

To my family and friends, they know who they are; I thank you and know that wherever you may be . . . my prayers are always with you. May you always walk into the light and follow a righteous path no matter how hard and dim it may seem. There is always a light at the end of the tunnel, don't ever believe otherwise. Stay always focused and positive and all will pass. After every storms, there follows a hidden rainbow waiting to be captured, seen and explored. Please catch it before it goes. Life is beautiful when you learn to be at ease . . . and feel it goes this ease.

To my precious son, James, My Sir, my Lighting Knight, and rod; you're the reasons for my living and you're my miracle. I am so very proud of you. To my husband, Jose, through all of our ups and downs, I hope to see us always growing more in love together. Jet'aime beaucoup, French-"I love you". "Remember, we're this petal of a flower needing each other to survive. I've learned that you're right, loves does grow, and you just have to water it."

Minerva A. F. Garcia.

My poems consist of subjects that I feel are important to me at the moment. I am concerned with life, our environment and future generation, as well as the planet and our country and how we're reflected and influence each other. I am happily married and have a wonderful son. I try my best in all of my pursuits and try to encourage harmony despite what I might see, hear and read. It's difficult for me to remain at the moment and be focused. I want to reach out, touch the world, and keep it safe. There is so much destruction (physical, mental, societal and environmental). I want to see the world as a beautiful flower, not only through my writing, but perceive and preserve it from danger!

Minerva A. F. Garcia.

Angels Holding A Dove For You And I To Live

Spread your silent wings . . . You're being loved so much
You might not think so . . . You're high up above being love
There's nothing to be afraid of from the above . . . Its here you can't trust
as I ask?

Why it is man can't be trusted and lacks so much love?
I can sense angels are coloredily and so beautifully . . . All I trust
I am not insane but very intoned hearing recognizable tunes all fine—
Why man is so cruel and others with few ounce on their blood and back,
if weight a lot?

The truth exist in theirs egos that weights a lot
know-
The truth exist is their egos that weights a lot know that
THAT IN YOUR COFFINS . . .

You **can't** fit all your money and worldly possessions but you only can fit
love
Be glad to fit only LOVE for it is weightless and doesn't cost a cent!

*R*ejoice for being alive and don't fall back. Just pick yourself up
*A*im high reach for a dove and be amazed at
*G*od's grace for …He made all including us!
*R*espect all living, no matter what!
*H*e and we are one-He is all three
*H*e is not a mystery He is God—that we should learn to love
*H*e has so much to give . . . If only we could seek
*I*f we love him . . . We'll get so much
*L*ove is the strongest bond
*I*s free—It's always seeking
*I*t's a dove
*E*xplore it . . .
*D*on't wait for tomorrow
*L*et it be today
Who can wait?
Don't hesitate… Before is too late… this ride may not wait

An Interpretation of How Do I Love Thee of Elizabeth Barrett Browning (Sonnet 43)

How should she love? Counted all her ways . . .
With all of her breaths till there was none in sights or her sights of her heights
With an overwhelmed of her souls reaching abnormalities of uncontrollability sights
Search for a nothing but perfection without ever being erased
She loves with all her might of the days
Without any quarrels days and nights
She loves openly with an abundance of liberty, as all man should without any fights
She loves whitely with all saintly psalms
She loves with an un-crazy mood as she puts in good use
In her wrinkled days and her childhood awakes of innocence
She'll always love and defend this love to all its use
With a longing not finding her saints she'll continue to defend this love with all her breath
With a facial expression of laughter's and fears of her life as God choose
She will no doubt love even more after death as is more ... she'll endure

October 28, 2013, 10:00AM

How Do I Love Thee? (Sonnet 43) by Elizabeth Barrett Browning

How do I love thee? Let me count the ways.
I love thee to the depth and breadth and height
My soul can reach, when feeling out of sight
For the ends of being and ideal grace.
I love thee to the level of every day's
Most quiet need, by sun and candle-light.
I love thee freely, as men strive for right.
I love thee purely, as they turn from praise.
I love thee with the passion put to use
In my old griefs, and with my childhood's faith.
I love thee with a love I seemed to lose
With my lost saints. I love thee with the breath,
Smiles, tears, of all my life; and, if God choose,
I shall but love thee better after death.

God, I Can Prove

Part I
God is conceptual-
He lives in your heart and mind
Which one do you believe?
I believe-
He is the cell
He is the units of this cell
All celluarities begins and ends
All with Him…
Now, I want to test you
Do you've a pen?
Do you've a mind?
Do you comprehend in this tense and/or do you just pretend?

Part II
I tempt you to try-
To divide this union
That which has occurred
More than that occurred 3.5 and/or 4.8 billions?
It's all a chain of a command-
By that which you can't break
You can't create nor recreate
It's all a link of DNAs

Its genes that you can wear with blue jeans and/or no jeans
I believe He exists in more than that…
He is more than that-
He is this microscopic bit
He is that humongous of things
He is everything in all these… things

Part III
He is this unexplained first cell
He is the units of the alpha **(A or α)**
He is the structures of the omegas' **(Ω or ω)**
He is infinity symbol of ∞ that never ends
He is un-finity […], that which you can't explain that ends
Where does the first life form-
Comes from?
Who put the 1ˢᵗ cell?
Where creation came?
Who tried it-
To practiced?
Who mastered this
And indeed Okayed it?
He who is visible and invisible?
He who is the source of light?
He who is the provider of all the crops?
He who cares and is the maker
Thru love-
Of a perfect planet
As truly is
It is Earth

10/27/14 @ 6PM

What is . . . love?

Love is a hidden garden
All for the views . . .
Todos en la joventud-
Meaning all in the youth

When you plant a seed
With love-
You create a beautiful
Scenery . . . breathe for the taken

Is a hidden garden?
All man ought to see it
It's not hard to find it
You just have to seek it . . .

Where should you start?
Start in your heart for it's a work of art . . . for if you learn to listen to it
You'll find it . . . Gardens has its own language
Is the most beautiful work of art-

Can you be obedient?
And listen to it!
Can you take that?
Why not?

June 17, 2013

Love is . . .

Love
Is a flower
Is a *plant* . . . Is where Gods lives

Love
Is not a thorn
Is not a toy . . . It can be only put on by Him

Love
Perhaps described by some
It is a Rose

I say . . .
It is a heart to be grown . . . Waiting...to be

I say . . .
It is pink

Love
A burning fire
Waiting . . . To explode

Love
Are rainbows
Language all hearts understands…

Doesn't recognize Whiteout nor easers
Its paints all insides

Lives in all colors
Welcomes all races

Forgives all
Feels pains far from within… It's never vain
Loves is sacred

Love
Have all the strengths
It's powerful

Love-
Is a crystal seed… perhaps few see?
It's lovely:
It really nice to please
It's for all to grow

Love
Frees… All man from sins making one feels weightlessness
It's truly liberty in peace

It must be watered
It must be nurtured
It always waits for the right train for you to take for its so patient

It must live-
Expresses all that is good

Love stands tall and alone waiting for you…. To explore
Paints without ink and brushes your hair

Needs no words…. Are all silences at times?
Needing warmth from within…

Love is passion
From the Divine… its never blind nor burgess

Love there's eyes of endless beauty
Man shouldn't divide

It can leave a wound like your favorite perfume
Has the nicest of smell…letting you know times heals wants you back if
you've love

As it renews
All can cure…

Love is the calmest of all the seas that sees
It's a dove from the above

Love is a tiny tree…
Within letting man be breathing free

Love is new
Love warmth's without a fire

The warmth of the sun captured rainbows
The bluest of the skies are reflections… there lies horizon and a prism

Never give up-
Dream in colors if you can and remove all morbid images

Love is the strongest
Of all the bonds (-, =, ≡)

Love begins waiting to be… borne
Found in pink hearts

Love never ends, never dies …always seeks
Never wants to be alone for long…. Seeks the company of peace wanting
all man to live free

May 1, 2009

In The Microbiology Lab

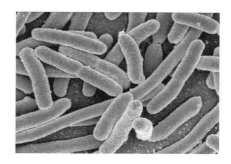

I am standing very still
No noise here
But I began to cry
At the sounds of the microbes
That I thought I heard. Melting fast-
Not wanting to die.
I experienced the death of an E.coli.
Shrinking, unpigmented and so,
Its colors just went by. Awake from your silly
Sleep E.coli-
Today is not your day
Too much pain you caused,
But today I'll bring you to life. Come from the dead
Old E.coli-
This is an old experiment
Today once again I'll bring you to life.

Thursday, January 02, 2003

Paper Frog

As we age,
We look into the mirror and agree upon
"We are lovable creatures in the nudes." Golden and silverfish too and
leaping Paper Frogs,
All seem to be with heavy years,
Our nostalgia increases with time,
And all that remains are shadows of youths. All must to an end,
Except for my Paper Frog
For has no heart. He knows no defense,
He is never offended,
For he never knew a friend.

Thursday, January 02, 2003

Ice Cream in the Sun

Music melts my heart
Like Ice cream in the sun
The soul feels all absorbed
By my musical listening of my responsive heart

As touch breathe by my skies-
I can't reach any diamond within my grasp
For all my mind wants to do
Is listen to soft melodies
As gently put me to sleep

As I awake, I want more music for my ears
So I can soothe them day and night
Pleasantly a sound without any quarrels

October 31, 2013

Appreciate Each Day

Make a difference each day-
Make it a business to take a business trip to be nice
Wear your best business suit if have too
Gather a meeting on your business trip

Don't feel silly-
It'll be sillier if you're mean with extremes
All you need in niceness is one suit
To accomplish all your pursuits

Take a stand with your finest suit
Let no man rule you
Since you rule your mind
Always be nice . . .

As said, "**Live Your Life as your Last**"
With that-
Know it can
Know better yet, you can change and create make a difference for you
and I today . . .

October 31, 2013

IN THE PARK

He may be old or young,
Seemingly sad or dreary,
Perhaps even dirty and confused,
As his rags tear apart by life's denies.

It is life put onto a bag,
But too heavy a burden,
For compassion was no match
And can't be touched—

By the love, he once had.
Trying to awake his empty heart,
Traveling very fast,
Noticing no pocket money—
Turned his back feeling lonely,
He questioned God,
"Does life have to be like this?"
He went to sleep in the park,

With newspapers for a blanket,
A picture of his baby daughter on his hands.
He never awoke, but was found
As a frozen flesh abandon.

This is life's mystery—
Now under the grace in the gates
Awaits the heaven for a man
"For sure, love will not deny this soul."

. . . OF A PLACE CALLED VALLEY

For where two or three
Are gathered in my name,
There am I in the midst of them.
Matt. 18:20

God does draw us near
He never gives more than we can dearly hold

With every rainbow that goes
He can understand our troubled heart

He can calm away our fears
Tornadoes may follow our paths

He's there to put away some broken pieces
That never seemed to fit

In despair and desperation
He can listen and put you to sleep

He triumph in every ways
In trials and pain, love and prayers makes you strong

Never deny his ways
For God's palm is not an empty valley

But an entrance to a founder's keepers
Of an everlasting faith of a place

His place is a valley
Where you can smile and be at ease

I love this place
Because is where I can fall asleep

A TRIBUTE

It was September 11 of this 2001
As 2,813 lost their lives
The World Trade Center gone
The skies opened that day
We all cried—
It was the saddest of the days
An American Airlines flight entered
Onto Tower 1 at 8:46AM
An inferno—All hopes gone
As the evil doers
Masterminded a horrendous crime
At 10:29 AM fell
We all cried
As Tower 2 followed
For sure was a very sad day
As will always be imprinted in our minds
As in the history throughout times
Today Ground Zero—
Remains a sacred place
There stands the proof, as is name

An eternal blue flame
A cross of steel stands today
A symbol of freedom
As citizens courage we praise
No doubt there remains
They lost their lives
Today we pray
There bears all the silent names
Their families' hurt
As their hearts not the same
Theirs is the lights of heaven
For sure no denies here—
For each holds a sacred name of love
A sacrifice as paid their lives
A tribute remains—
In Staten Island as Post Cards two angels wings at ease with the skies

An interpretation of Emily Dickinson Hope is the Thing with Feathers

By Minerva A. Garcia, MLS, MT (ASCP)[CM]

Hope is that holds that carries feathers as it weathers
That indeed pieces the inner depths
That contemplates the melodies without a song
It never endures as is tall,
The nicest of laughter are the bursting of sounds;
The bitter storm must be
By which could put to shame a birdie
That increases its body temperature so strong.
I've heard the frozen of the valleys
The mystery of the unsound dead seas,
For even within an exaggerations,
I question a loaf of bread that comes for me

Hope is the Thing with Feathers

By: Emily Dickinson

"Hope" is the thing with feathers
That perches in the soul
And sings the tune without the words
And never stops at all,

And sweetest in the gale is heard;
And sore must be the storm
That could abash the little bird
That kept so many warm.

I've heard it in the chillest land
And on the strangest sea,
Yet never, in extremity,
It asked a crumb of me.

El Don And Sanch

Don Quixote
How you aimed to be a knight
Undeterred by age or pain

Is not absurd
To save the world from evil deposition

We may not be
Ready to comprehend such a man

Why are you lost in illusion?
Has life left you dissatisfied?
Have you become blind?
Man errs at all times?

There is wisdom to this adventure
As seen by Sancho Panza
Life dies but great works are eternal

The flame of times comes
Runs with the skies
Unable to match

The winds come and goes back and forth in every season
The waves as turtledoves love to swim with it
Are you ready for it?

A MICROBE

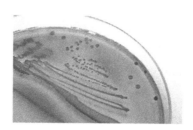

Part I (1)
What is it?
That which I wish money can multiple
But multiplies when it replicates
Every 20 minutes as 2 is 4 now 8, 16, 32, 64, 128, 256, 512, 1024, so on . . .
Now u've over 100,000,000s of new destructive cells
Desperately trying to get under your deep skin
This visitor you don't want next to next of kin

Part II (2)
A bacterium
A tiny living thing
Unicellular—
A microscopic piece
An almost invisible living thing
That occupies a little piece
So often likes to cause disease
And just want to be like this . . .
With its flagella and/or none . . . for propulsion and/or pili for
attachment as have appendages
It knows how to move and attach to a being
Should we question its existence—
Its been here before man 4.8 billions of years

Part III (3)
Why question?
Because often is the case to invade
As an unfriendly in nature a host it needs to live to cause disease
It just wants to be . . . and loves to spread
Micro
Be
Well that its prefix and suffix and strives in smallness
Is there a way can defend—it is so potent even with its bits
Being like seen only through the naked eyes
The shapes varies
The color varies
The disease varies as humans they leave in cries
And I say to investigate, "Why they just like to perform this why?"

Part IV (4)
Perhaps it may be of:
An aerobe, loves O2
An anaerobe can't stand O2
A facultative anaerobe grows either way with O2 or no CO2
Aerotolerant poisoned by O2
An obligate anaerobe, starvation of O2
A microaeophillic grows @ 42
A halophile loves salt

Part V (5)
A simple friendly . . . Staph as is StaCoNeg barely onto skin a
normalflora, ok a bug
An MRSA, pathogenic GERM as is Methicillin Resistant Staphylococcus
Aureus
How it increase its resistance(R) as I theorized in '94 to Dr.Albino at
Wagner College
Predisposition of infections: VRE with a MRSA
Mechanisms: Both carries vanA gene
"It was the vanA gene transferred of plasmids from VRE onto the MRSA
lead VRSA/
VRE, EnterococcusVanco R gene Transfer onto Staph gene thru its
transposon '94"

VRE→(VRE + MRSA)→E: VancoR + Staph:Van S→Enterococcus
VanAtransfer Staph→Now a Staph Vanco R could be (hVISA, VISA, VRSA)
All due to antimicrobial therapy of great lengths . . . How long?
Some thought I was mad and I theorized I was not-
I proofed all wrong as witnessed truth in
1996: Japan in May1st case of VISA came to exist . . .
2002: Michigan and PennsylvaniaVRSA
2004: New York 1 case Michigan 3 cases
2009: New York once again til now all 17 in USA
Followed by France, England and HongKong
=4-8 ug/ml, VISA
≥16 ug/ml, VRSA
E-Test of a gradient of MICs would detect subpopulations of Rs called "SVS"

Part VI (6)
A hVISA (MRSA), a heteroresistantStaph
A VISA (MRSA), a vancointermediate Staphor GISA
A VRSA, vanco resistant Staph
A VRE, vanco resistant Enterococcus
Or could be hVISA (MSSA) as I encountered in a diabetic surgical wound 2010
VISA (MSSA) or VRSA lacking MecA gene
A MDRO, a multi-drug resistant organism as is

Part VII (7)
An ESBL, an extended spectrum beta lactamase
A-Metallo BL-1, a New Delhi NDM-1,class B enzyme needs presence of zinc strikes activityCreating resistances of an E.coli by a BL ABXs, as class A, characterized by its Hydrolytic mechanisms
This includes: Penicillinases&Cephasporinases TEM, SHV, and CTX-M
Does not hydrolyze carbapenems at all
Now Class A with: BL & a carbapenemase
Acts encoding chromosomes (chromosomal encoded enzymes) or
Plasmids encoded includes all of these:
SME(S.marcescens enzyme)
NMC (non-metalloenzymecarbapenemase)
IMI (imipenem hydrolyzing BLs)

ID'ed among isolateEnterobacter
KPC (Klebsiella pneumonia carbapenemase) by plasmid encoded enzymes
GES (Guiana extended spectrum) in K.pneumonia and
P.aeruginosaThese are all major blows for too many of souls
Theirs are unusual GNR like a MHT+, carbapenemase producerErtapenam as the indicator
Danger creeps in under the bed as nosocomial bugs tries to attack as a class A, B and D Where resistance enters in thru mechanism: impaired permeability due porin mutations

Part VIII (8)
LF and/or NLF
An oxidizer
A pigmented or unpigmented
Dimorphic fungi
A gram positive
A gram negative
A cocci
A rod and/or bacilli
A diplococci
A pleomorphic
A gram variable
A branching mini creature
A spirochete like Borrelia could exist . . . like this

Part IX (9)
Yeast as is Candida albicans and C. dubliniensis
A mold as Aspergillous blackness as it exists
Coccidioidomycosis with skin tumors
Amphoteracin B or the azoles ketoconazole or itraconazole treats
Dust storms could be its welcoming environmental to be . . .
Histoplasma whiteness likes to be as dimorphic a fungi be-

Part X (10)
Now this pathogenic bug that caught my eyes not under the rug but Columbia Univ.
Was *"Mobiluncusmulieris"* in '84
My fastidious research Micro bug in '04

Gr+ @ no presence of O2& CDC ANA, CDC w/ KV & 5% BAP w/ TSA
Divides anaerobic cell
Not like your typical ANA growing 2 days this takes the cake for takes 5-7 days
With its super ultrastructure of gram variability
With its discharges/abscess and biofilms as its known doesn't likes to be film
Its strives to lives PH ≥ 4.5
Has chosen a weak/fragile candidates
O' dreadful that loves to strikes as increased WBCs
Microscopic key ID of BV—increased on its Clue cells
Bacterial Vaginosis disease
With its polar flagella it attaches
By tumbling motility macromorphological as Listeria monocytogenes
Both being Ninhydrin +, BH+
Listeria catalase+
Mobi L-Proline-Amino-Peptidase activity+ as is C.dubliniensis

Part XI (11)

Too odorous as an unfriend, enters as it attaches to the vaginal cells
Why prefer pregnant female to befriend?
With microbial pathogenesis in existence by hemolysis, lysing the cells toxins it is . . .
Indeed an unwelcome friend creeps in . . . .
Let's now let MD treat: Clindamycin and/or Metronadazole
Mechanisms: Clinda bactericidal
And Metro cytotoxic

Part XII (12)

O'How?
By freeing radicals to the toxic cells
Interacting to the host cells
DNAs strands breaks
Sure this lead to a fatal blow
As destabilization of DNA helix
This is the realizationinward-
Now can be seen decay of inactive end products
For sure-
Death is now entering in-creeping all of them

Killing of the bugs
To treat or not could be the keys?

Part XIII (13)
To avoid rupture of the membranes
An early child-birth
A pre-mature labor
An unsurprised cry as is a miscarried
These lives must be saved!!!
This was a microbial pathogenic who likes to bug humans in their acts
Who can no longer ease to be . . .

Part XIV (14)
There so many mores . . . Too many to question
I start with an airborne as droplets in the air
Aerosols as they just escaped from humans inside thru their breath/
respi-air
An acid-fast like TB
As it loves to exists . . . and it triumphs always
But wait . . . it is fast like MTB, grows fast?
MD come defends this unfriend
Elaborate they're
Evolving they always . . . with its mechanisms
They tend to win
Then again man of science comes in with an antibiotic
To kill this unfriendly bug
But they always try to survive and fight
For always wants to remain an unknown

Part XV (15)
There's viruses, can it be grab as a BT by extremes? Let's not go there . . . !
Hola, not for Ebola (EBOV or EVD)-
Hemorrhagic fever leaving-draining its victims as they bleed
How begin to treat? Research drug
ZMapp by BioTechMappBioPharmaceuticals, Inc
Works by controlling the continuous increase of its symptoms
Man shouldn't be left in cries, pains, defamed thru death as viral loads
comes to claim

Part XVI (16)

In the Congo of Africa entered in '76
Peeling people's under skin . . .
It is truly Black Death or the Red Plague?
An unwanted visitor quietly swamped in: 1976, '07, and '92 extending '14
Hosts are:Bats, monkeys, gorillas and who else knows . . .
Transmission: Exposure of contaminated viral loads
Could had crept in thru touch, salivary glands
Possible came to be thru a broken skin (abrasions), digestion
Of meats and/or uncooked of these indelicacies
That people couldn't see was not a good treat!
Contacts with: Infected BFs, animals dead or undead
Symptoms: Fever, sore throats, muscle aches, headaches
Followed by:Vomiting, diarrhea, rush, cough, low
BP now dec liver fction depleting all their internal fluids
Victims of 90% are sent to their unwanted homes-
In terrors and visible horrors a cemetery now they called "HOME"

Part XVII (17)

It came "WITH NO STOP"—to spread:
With no guinea pigs, in Guinea
Sir in, Sierra Leone
Not actor Steve Seagal, in Senegal
Neither, but all in Nigeria
Some pain, in Spain
We feelings of uncontrolled train seeing images of its victims, arriving in
the USA
Also, not in the wallet but, in Mali
Thru the hands in France
No way, In Norway
Not with Swiss cheese but in Switzerland
United all in the kingdom, in United Kingdom

Part XVIII (18)

A bite on your deep skin could be a key . . .
Deadly stage: Advanced disease as fever creeps in $\geq$ 101.2
Now you all need full coverage head-toe
To stop the multiplications of this viral
You can't run but be a prisoner

By a microscopic creature known as a "Microbe"
With so many loads . . . viral loads trucking all

Part XIX (19)
Today as it stands it was WHO, who states:
Deaths of 6,460 out of 17,290 by Dec 1st
It's a Flovirus, family of HIV
Now u know how deadliest it is
Emile Ouamouno Dec' 2013 introduced a huge toll
Him mom, sister, grandmother all he took to his tomb
In the village of Meliandu
In its quiet not as a crow in the silence . . .
Who knows?
Now known as EVD
Not an unknown has come in to claim lives

Part XX (20)
For sure now, who comes and credits the lab? It is a **"Licensed Clinical
Laboratory Professional"** who comes thru the silence as a hero being
discriminated not by the Gods but by pay not by fate?
**Who rescues the patients by ID'ing all the microbes! Yet, doesn't
claim to be a hero** . . . at 20th it ends with few microbiological friends.
These Techs are just happy to know, they can make a difference always to
Bring the unknowns known to man . . .

AN AMERICAN SOLDIER

Part I.
The land of freedom we stand
This soldier of an American soil lands
Fighting for peace and for his land
Come free this man from pains
He will always stand tall looking for someone
To aid and alleviate all their pains
Away from home and his patriots too
For wants to live not insane but free from pains
If ever, question this man, "Why such deeds my friend?"
He will reply, "Man should never live like this!
Why explain?
I see at times we can be insane, and who are we to blame?"
"Fathers of the heavens, wherever you may be, listen . . .
We all want to breathe a little free
Teach us to learn to be like this and be at peace
Moreover, would be no need for soldiers to be . . .
We tried to reach and seek others some freedom
But instead, they slapped me and placed it on their back
For they buried peace on their yard
For they think never existed and cannot be now . . .
I shall fight until there'll be peace
Because I believe in me and no one

Can take that away from me
I am an American soldier
Who by rights?
Do constitute to certain beliefs
We are free?
I shall be at peace

Part II.
The American flag is to testify
My beliefs-
Til the day I die
My flag will be with me
Its has the colors of this flag especially red matching my blood
I know it-
For been buried in my inners of my hearts... of colors Red, White and
blue my arteries
My flag will be bury
...along with me
My mom and dad
Any offspring that I may off had
The future wife I may off had any yet is not known
I place it and buried it all in my soul...
I do hope man will never learn nor know
What I value most of all...
That is my home sweet home
America the Great is my piece of pie
I will say it again-
My mom and dad
Who always believed in me!
I know they will always still believe in me
Does our country

Do stand by me?
Do I care?
What do you ask of me?
I see the bravest of men not stand
Yet their head stands regardless if they're blind
Are the not blind that are-
Man of the world, you do stand today…tomorrow who knows
Give soldiers some peace by respecting their stands for they always try to
stand even on their hands
If they can…

Part III
If you ever begin to question this soldier-
Why do you try to stand without any legs and so….?
Why you've no hands?
He'll simply try to state regardless with half his tongue
I fought for you to stand today…
But I really don't care what you say
Because-
I am a free soldier
Who has allowed it to be?
Thru my own will
I was born to lead man
I've fought to be…
I know
I am free
I know more than that
I've died for you
I've died for me
I've died for man to be born
I've died to free man…

I've died for all
I died the day you deny a Vet
I really would die for any US soil man
I die a blank man stain in blood with my SS ID
Oh 'no not I…

Part IV
I may be stained in blood as a man
But I did free myself
I know I love all my fellow man
I can now die-
For am truly free
I can sense the spirits leaving me
I can stately feel all the ghostly views leave
I can see people say goodbyes
I can leave all beyond behind?
Who can fight like I?
I must leave all to the offsprings' I never had
I now will go to meet my maker and my creator
Who is now waiting for me?
I am excited to this meet
I've no regrets-
I've lived my life
As all soldiers should
I've fought all the battles
Leaving prints of me-
Despite what may others think of me
I am an America soldier with a flag
I leave a white, blue and red flag
That I allowed no one to grab-
Don't you ever let any one!
These are the reasons lost all of my hands
Now I know-
I can die more than just free…
I can only now grab onto to God for he sees man with no hands

Minerva A. Garcia, MLS, MT (ASCP)CM

DEPRESSION

I.

Is not madness an
Episode of a conflict?
Is just an earthly desire?
To let all else go trying
To reach a perfect state of the soul
Feelings of no return,
With your mind entering
A state of total darkness.
What can one do to escape?
Should you search for
A light, reach for a hand
Find rescue under some arms
Commune with your soul.

II.

If you search
For it...
It's worth more than gold
Keep digging
You'll strike not silver
I guarantee-
You'll definitely find
Your lost gold
Your mind may seem heavy
But is the oceans that are heavier
Enlighten your mind (s)...
Do you mind?
Enter onto the bluest of the skies and take a ride...
Discover to like it
You can exit a fresh-
You just learned to take deep fresh air...and breaths

HATRED

Don't we run through the same blood?

Whether black or white, yellow or tan,
Does not matter to the bones or the tones!

Hatred is a bad seed and an ugly emotion.
It doesn't allow the soul to be at ease but allows one to bleed

Stops peace allowing only the veins to swell and not breathe
Hatred is a dreadful scar that does not wear a scarf.

It makes one feel unloved and it's an empty bridge.
It allowing no one to cross the other side.

For it's a cemetery in all its un-extraordinary.
Please do not let be you or those you know and love

It takes away your smile and those around you
Who believes in you, keep away from it. . . Erase it!

Shield yourself and built a bridge of love.
If not, you will feel unloved, unwanted and dreadful

When they play this game, avoid and not play by it
If not, we will be destroyed.

Do not join the crowd and be just you.
Look at the mirror; see beauty besides you.

And flowers growing inside you of inner peace-
So love prevail all around and all that exists is more love

Deep within that's love-
Do not deny your heart(s) and beautiful mind of beauty . . .

Life is a constant goal waiting to explore-
So, let us catch it with the suns as each morning as it rises.

WTC SEPT 11

It seems like a dream
Almost unable to sustain
The symbol it stood
The finance center of the world
Our freedom was in question
Nevertheless, no doubt is freedom
We will search for a goal
As Americans would like to awake not
On this Sept 11
The burning flames
Steels collapsing
The cries that never survived
Our prayers stand
As families waiting I thank God twice
93 and 2001—
Not my family time as they survived twice
I know this is not a dream but live scenes
Created by monsters
Leaving horrendous scenes
Of silence and extremes

All left in our silent minds
That so often cries
America o'how beautiful of liberty we stand
Strong in all directions
In salvation
Will survive
Will strive
As these men took away out steel of towers
But our faith in liberty and heroes
Will always stand and remain strong
As our faith and hope endures and sustains us all

An interpretation of Edgar Allan Poe— A dream

A Dream—
In the fore tales of the future nites
I've foreseen the happiest of days gone—
But living a dream of water and luminescence
By which due me cracked and empty-hearted.

To they whose looks so sad contrast
For all seemed with him an arrow of sunburst
Turning back on all the clocks?
Its ok . . . to question and know
Dreams of misfit by daylight.

For the sacred of foresees for is what can be, foreseen
Even if all is revoked in this universal place,
There applauses me to a beautiful sunray of beam

A quiet angels stands by lighting the way echoing me splendidly.

Oh' luminescence thru the violence of the winds in dark,
Shaking from a rocket distance in the skies-
For it stands to ask why fixed shining white lights
In assertions by true faith-is a star?

By: Minerva A. Garcia

A Dream
by Edgar Allan Poe

In visions of the dark night
  I have dreamed of joy departed—
But a waking dream of life and light
  Hath left me broken-hearted.

Ah! what is not a dream by day
  To him whose eyes are cast
On things around him with a ray
  Turned back upon the past?

That holy dream—that holy dream,
  While all the world were chiding,
Hath cheered me as a lovely beam
  A lonely spirit guiding.

What though that light, thro' storm and night,
 So trembled from afar—
What could there be more purely bright
 In Truth's day-star?

When You Plant A Seed With Love

Plant a seed with love
You'll see it grow

Plant a seed with love
You'll see a beautiful garden multiple

Plant a seed of love
You'll witness food from the above

Plant a seed with love
You'll witness birds and bees smells God's treats

Plant a seed with love
You'll feel your eyes harmonize with picturesque of grace

Plant a seed of love
You'll not be sad for long for it's a wishful view in youths

Plant a tree of love

You'll feel your heart grow inches and your senses with immensities

Plant a tree of love
It's your heart . . . that it'll thank you for the feelings of lightness that
You've a heart
Plant a tree of love

Not yesterday, Not tomorrow but Today . . . for tomorrow you'll have
Bountiful fruits

October 31, 2013

The Love of A Flower

Love is peace without thoughts
Is a colorful flower
Is a blue light
Is a view all in youth . . . . Love is a hidden star
Is a moon yet to be discovered
Is a honeymoon onto his deep skin
Is the hunger of man to be loved eternally. The love of a flower . . . .
Is a rest upon your man's chest
Is a first love of a Springtime dream
Is a gift from the above onto his arms. The love of a flower . . . .
Is to witness the birth of your son
Is to awake for the first time
Is to swim for love once again with him. The love of a flower . . . .
Is to really learn to love and see life for what it is
Is to be able to write a poem to the sky and smile
Is to look at your love and state "Indeed you're all my youth"

Thursday, January 02, 2003

The Role of Poet

By no means
Am I a genius of words,
But I do attempt to write my pen with multitudes
Of love to defend this love found in my deep heart. Poems I stately write
For the purpose to reach the human soul.
I may not be right at times
But I am satisfied to release the contents-
May the subjects that are in my minds
Possibly antonyms and synonyms to my beliefs
As is all silence. The truth exist
To convince this mind,
That the lines to these prints
Are well defined as other question. To reach a goal that is,
To speak softly and silently.
Just let the pen, my mind and my paper
Work with me as God gently listens and caresses me.

Thursday, January 02, 2003

9/11 Reflections: Minerva Garcia Feeling helpless while praying for her brother-in-law

Staten Island Advance/Anthony DePrimoMinerva
Garcia is thankful her family was spared.
(Staten Island Advance/Anthony DePrimo)

I recall that day of Sept. 11, 2001, so vividly. I was working at Beth Israel Medical Center, NYC, in the Microbiology Department, attending to my patient's lab report . . .

All of a sudden, I hear one of my colleagues shout, "Turn on the radio, the WTC has been hit by a plane . . ."

I got a phone call from my husband a few minutes later: "Are you hearing what is happening to the WTC? My brother works in one of those towers . . ."

My sister-in-law also called worried . . . I made it my business to be strong and stay focused for the family. I said a special prayer . . .
As I approached the window from the 12th floor of the laboratory, I remembered seeing the thick smoke rising out. I was praying for my brother-in-law at all times . . .

I had the intentions of running in desperation and trying to help. But our hospital's administration would not allow any emergency staff to leave their post and I know they saved my life. I wanted to go out there and see what I could do to help.

My husband was dismissed earlier from his teaching job in Brooklyn and my son, who was in elementary school, was also let go and picked up by his grandfather.

It was a bit chaotic for the whole family not knowing where my brother-in-law was. When the family got a phone call from my brother-in-law, WG, you could sense the relief.

As I walked out of the lab for a break, I recalled people walking like zombies and motionless along First Avenue at East 17th street . . . Then, I saw people coming to our ER asking if their loved one was brought to our hospital.

I was so sad and feeling so utterly helpless that I didn't know what to do. I started to write and submitted some of my poems to the Staten Island Advance and my union. I assisted my church pastor at Sacred Heart in West Brighton as best as I could. I wrote poetic lines and framed them and they were distributed to families during a ceremonial mass . . .

Today, even more, as I look back, I thank God for giving us the second Chance with my brother-in-law and sparing us from so much pain . . .

The Supreme

Each passing day
I begin to understand
Why he is the majesty
And holds such supremacy
He is the tallest tree
He is the deepest sea
He is those tranquil clouds
For he is the supreme
We rarely seek him
He is our substance
He lets us see
He is the shining sea
He is those mountains
He is those crops and flowers
He is glory in the heavens
For he is the supreme

The Words of The Lord

Part I

The words of the Lord
Is the kindest
Is the divinest
Is all that matters here
Is the only rule to live by
Is not chaotic here
Is where man can live free
Is a place that is safe
Is all peace without extremes
Is not a mystery but plentiful trees
Is a paradise all in the skies
Is a river that flows within
Is a sweet gentle loving song with rosy alleluia
Is a toy put onto your hands being rock by the divine
Is a note you once missed for no ears you had
Is a gentle gesture letting you know He cares
He is all you need
He is the spirit of all
He is life satisfying all sounds and souls
He treats one like a dove, making you feel gold, this is He.

Part II
He is the master of all peace…
He is the bluest of all the lights
He is the holder of what is all love
He holds the keys to life…
He is life satisfying what is to live
Life is a cell… the units of microscopic piece of all we
This is all He
A piece of the all this universe intertwine
Past, present and future generations
He is a mutation and/or he may not
He is perfect
Even though you may not
He's creation-
Despite you may think not
He has so many eyes
Here, there and everywhere
He climbs without hands, walk without feet, speak without tongue, hears
without ears
He is so much in one
He sees all without eyes
He senses all without a body
He smells without a nose
He's the tallest of all the mountains
He gives the finest of crops- Perhaps bleeding for all our love

Part III
He moves with invisible wings
He breaths without a heart
He holds everyone's heart
He understands everyone's heart
He may be or not in likeness as us
He loves man so much-
He allows us to start every day anew
This I do know-
He truly loves all of us
He always fights for us
He holds you when you may think not
He's your defender
He's your best of friend
You will know this-
The very moment you allow Him to enter
You'll never be the same
For you've discover an everlasting true friend…
Who will never betray you-
For He has always fought for you and I
He also bled…
You've passed his test
The moment you accepted Him in
Now don't you ever look back!

The Journey of a Rainbow
By Minerva A. Garcia

There rainbows all our lives
They appear in different colors
We may not see them with our naked eyes
We may not know it exists
This rainbow is God, He's all around us
His message is love; His colors are the heart and a breath
As confusion persists upon this Earth
He surrounds us with love
We must learn to walk away from it for what is not
The key is master your inner strengths—that is Divine
Just let all peace within prevail
Silence is the language of love
Whisper unto your friends there might be just one
It's okay if you've none
Its better no company than a bad one
Believe deep within, for you're guided by spiritual energies
Nothing is hidden for clouds disappearing…

Left are the breezes in your deep and responsive heart
All the grays disappeared as love filled all the gaps-
Perhaps laughter's of an immense as rains have come, erased all your pains
The sun once again shines and a rainbow stands journeying home
Filling all your hearts with more love
Truly-
Explain what love is?

Challenge

Challenge is facing obstacles and never giving
Up—
Is combating a disease and rising each morning with the sun
With a smile
Is comforting those in distress even if you're there
And are realizing you're human but that you can give a loving hand

Is loving your fellow man even though there is none for you,
Is getting wet for no umbrella are in your hands

And is opening your heart and filling your soul with love
Is giving hope and strength to those who lack

Is being kind and sharing yourself with those
In need—
Is searching for peace where there is none and is to seek
Liberty and live harmoniously despite what you might see
But to stand by your beliefs—

To challenge the court for the truth is a view, for God,
The innocent why there is crime—
To question the Unbelievers, evil doers, the pessimists and or not could
be the key—
The beauty exists when you believe keep it like this,
Breath free and rest in peace

Depleted Rose

Life is not sad
For God meant not
Is always blissful
For there is a sun
Guiding the son

Let's not
Deplete this rose
Tomorrow may be gone
Life is not sad
Here comes the sun

Don't feel defeated
You can't bleed
You are a rose
Not a thorn
But born

Free . . .
Will carry
You on

Petals

We—
Are like petals of a flower
Needing each other to survive
We're unlike any color
We're all colored all in one
Why Fight—
If no struggle exists
No need to exist for a fight
We'll all survive
Life much as ought to be . . .

Rose Garden

Why is it the roses along with its petals?
Is immensely beautiful for most eyes

Why is it-
No matter what colors is still pleasant for the human eyes

Why is it-
Red is beyond unique to satisfied even the most depressed vision

Why do I question this?
For no matter what color, a rose along with its petals creatures beauty to the eyes

You can grow it in your garden
You can admire it from a distance or close

You can give it as a gift
You can… if you love someone or not

You water it with love
Before you give it-

You'll get a response and yield a nice look
A smell so unique and so you'll get a thanks...

There may be colors of Red, Yellow, Pink, White, orange, purple
And any colors you may wish to make it all your own

Each individual petal has a message-
For you and the one you love

A rose is nothing without each other-
There are petals making all one beautiful rose

I prefer red, for matches my blood and my unique heart
I also content with pink so can match my pink heart....

I can look at it-
As most women tend to like pink probably for its feminity

When I do get one-
I will look at it... Smell and nicely water onto a vase

I feel complete-
As I know it's a treat from God to me being so truly a gift from the above
to me

UNIQUENESS

Unlike any we seen
No matter what they say
In our eyes is all that matters
Quality so different
Unable to accept others opinions
Eyes of yours is all that matters
Note that only kind words you'll accept
Excellent and exceptional qualities you'll accept
Sure are its demands…
Seriously, is all you'll ever understand for all its **uniqueness**?

Love is . . . If Is free—it doesn't cost a thing

I

Is Love ever wrong?
You don't need to advertise it
You want to seek it where it exist

The key for anyone to search for it
May you find the whisper?

It shouldn't be too far . . .
It's a hint for you to start to look for it

Love never dies-
It never runs out of style

It's always searching for peace without extremes
Is always real unlike anything you'll ever known

It is for real-
It is a dream but with plentiful trees

It's a gentle breeze letting you know you exist
It's a powerful blow of rain falling gently upon your face
Its man searching for himself-
This is truly real

Can you take more?
I dare you to run and leave Love behind

Whoa . . . Is this for real?
Is a forest being burn and you not turning off the fire as nature screams

Why you letting me burn?
What acts of injustice have I done to deserve to disappear?

I may not come back, but it's the mark I'll leave that is real!
I was all pack as man turned their backs… In order for me to crack

What tree am I?
Oak or maple?
I say I know and you don't, can you stomach that!

II
Why does man do that?
Indeed are all cruel acts not all intact

Why is all man not black?
Why have they been persecuted for their skin?

Why they've thought they've no brains?
It's the White man turning peoples' back and giving them many bags
Pack

I can't begin to explain why men are so vain
When they all share the same veins

All colored red looking blues for the view
White man, what an ugly perfume?

Whoa . . . a smell of prejudice I have no taste
I only like my define by "I" as Love

Can you ever match that?
Do I make myself clear?

How do you see the glass?
Is it empty and/or do I have to view you to conclude a view

It is the ugliest of perfumes as cracks my good bones-
I now must seek an orthopedic to explain why man

Has cracked my good bones
Can you listen softly as the waterfalls falls gently

Expressing to nature I am here to stay
But, I beg you please, let no man know this!

I can't explain why men are all so vain?
They surely can't feel pain

What creature are they, who seek to escape?
Why so desperately they put the weights on others and theirs now feels
light?

III
Why man don't want to learn to navigate their partakes?
I tell take your heavy weights to the air, dare you, it might not feel it

I question again-
What is all this air? I might find the time to inflate

The balloons are flying high along with the kites
Are they friends?

Flying high trying to reach the skies
Like Daedalus an architect, inventor and

An old mythology master of craftsmanship
Indeed building artificial wings for himself and his

Son Icarus-
His native land Athens as coincidental my name of the Romans as is, Minerva

Oh, what a shame you brought Daedalus
As you did portray a cruel act- How do you react?

Daedalus you feared that the boy (your dear son)
Would surpass your in talent

There by, you committed a cruel act
Why . . . Why . . . Why may I ask? Were you on crack?
And/or why did you crack?

I forgot not the style in the era of the Gods-
Daedalus you Cowardly feared that the boy would surpass you in talent

Why did you murder him in a cruel act?
By tossing him from the Acropolis of Athens-
The lands of the Gods

You must pay for these acts
And be tried by the Areiopagus,

Ancient Greek court—
Now you banished from your dear home, city of Athens.

Since Minos controlled the sea around Crete
Now, no route of escape there, Daedalus seeks only way out, by air-

That I say-
This Why?

IV

To really escape and/or escape, Daedalus built wings for himself and
Icarus (his most unfortunate of son's)

He whose dearly and
Beloved purest and surest of son

Put together by feathers..and oh'yes, tightly with wax
Daedalus warned his son not to fly too close to the sun for he knew for
sure,

Would melt his wings—
Not a philosophical guess I may say

Not too close to the sea,
Know for would dampen them and make it hard to fly.

He flew from Crete, all so excitedly
He being careless.

Flying close too the sun god Helios.
There it was, waxes holding together his wings

As melted from the heat needing a defeat?
… after heat

He fell to his death, drowning in the sea
Did he fall to his death?

Declaring defect?
Oh'yes he did onto the sea, sure he did

What a sad ending for a man
For infinitely, who aimed-reach too high . . .

The Icarian Sea, where he fell,
Was named after him to fulfill philosophy and history

Onto the Icarian Sea he felt-
Indeed was named after him

It was said-
As Heracles (Hercules) went by

A burial he provide
To stand the test of all times...

Oh, God dear...all stretched out
Daedalus lamented his unawaken son... feelings of blackness

Nearing Sicily, as came to court of Cocalus.
A place called Camicus, well let me tell you there's'

More as been said— myths suggest
Icarus drowned as he and his father attempted to swim to freedom, or so…

As that they built a boat and sailed away
Only to have it capsize—

Leading to the death of Icarus.
I prefer the "escape by air" version.

Icarus drown as he and his dad tried to escape
To tempt to swim

In search of freedom…
To sail among the deepest of seas

A boat they built,
Oh so sure to sail and go away

Don't you wish that Icarus
Had listened to his father?

Remember; if you aim too high
You'll fall break your bones…perhaps and all

Like Humpty Dumpty who had a great fall, too many pieces to put back,
I am so sorry now you can't react. Is a dear lesson to learn, don't crack not
even with drugs.

Don't be a fool—
Don't break your back

You'll never come back
Once you are dead

It's the end!
You'll miss so much.

I know of anyone
Who lost their lives' and came back

You don't want to know
If you'll ever be the first

It'll almost certain to be a lost bet
Just aim to be all intact... No need to react

For CR II Mom

I am so deeply sorry to learn of your loss. We will keep your family in our prayers during these difficult times. Rest assures, that the Lord will be looking down guiding and comforting you. May you put your strength in Him and seek his comfort for only He can give that. Our son, James, my husband Jose and I would like to express our most sincere condolences for your loss. Keep your faith strong and always lead on the Lord—for He is the answer. I'll be praying for your family to get through these moments of sorrows . . . special novenas and masses will be accompanied.

—Minerva A. Garcia May 17, 2011 Staten Island Advance

An Outstanding Service Of half a Century in the Laboratory

An activator and motivator
Laboratorian of a half a century
Accessible and accommodating to all the labs
*No doubt is **Alan**...*

Joking or not, he has mastered so much...
Always pleasant to work with and we know that
By his rules, he stood the test of times... without ever fallen behind
Laboratory standards he followed with demands and as he stands
Orders are his commands...
Never out of step ... with wisdom he championed onto the unknowns
Sir Alan, you've earn our respect
Kind to all his colleagues and he holds the keys
You've earned your laboratory distinctive wings ... and we expect you to fly
high today with honors well deserve , many wishes and congratulatory are the
demands because today you 've worked for it...

Nov 19, 2014 @ 5PM

A Retirement Wish For A Very Special Lady—Donna

There are people . . . but you're one of a kind.

There are people we come across in our lives
For certain reasons . . .

There are people who come across in our lives
That we don't know why . . .

There are people we come across in our lives
When we cry inside and only they can see this . . .

There are people who come across in our lives
To make known . . . . They been there and do care . . .

There are people who come across in our lives
Who are so nice . . . and this I do know why . . .

There are people we come across in our lives
Who are angels walking by and this . . . is you.

I am glad-
You and I crossed paths in our lives

Good luck
Be well… Enjoy your retirement

—*Minerva A. Garcia 12/1/13*

Whiteout I

I've to thank **President Barack Obama** for inspiring me with my creative literate art.

I was inspired thru his Bio I observed while watching **Larry King Live**... I had given

Writing poetry up and so, I was inspired thru his life being raised by a single Mom from

Kansas and dad being African, I was moved-

That I got busy and starting writing poems: Surely immediately and this was one. This I

Forward to his campaign and made a contribution- I knew then that he would be our next

President! I made it my business to have my son present and witness history made:

"The first African American President in US soil-

That an **inauguration of Barack Obama** as the **44th President** of the United States was dated to test and mark history and time...

For sure was day of **Tuesday, January 20, 2009.**

I felt more than content as a citizen!" He seems to be walking on waters, is he Moses?

For others he may not be... I know nothing sticks to him, regardless if others fallen next to him.

He never stands alone seems God been watching, blessing and protecting all along ...

I do not follow . . .
I do not lead
I am all silence
But for the Gods.

I am not a *plant*
I do need waters
I do need the *sun*
But most of all, I need love
To be *free* . . .
To be at ease
I do bleed . . . I do not scar
I do forgive . . . I do not like
To look back

I like to erase, but not with Whiteout
I like to paint and see beautiful rainbows
If I can, I would grow love and water it . . .

Love . . . Erases all
Lives in all colors and welcomes all races
Love forgives all
And restores faith . . .
Love never dies . . .
Never ends . . .
True love no need to defend
For never bends . . .

It's an open language for all man to comprehend-
It's the only language all colored hearts understands . . .

Fall 2008

Whiteout II

I like to ease but not with WHITEOUT
If only life could erase like WHITEOUT

I do not follow . . .
I do not lead
I am all silence
But for the Gods.

I am not a *plant*
I do need waters
I do need the *sun*
I DO NOT LIKE TO SCREAM
I'VE NEVER CARRY A GUN, am present without one

But most of all, I need love
To be *free* . . .
To be at ease
I do bleed . . . I do not scar
I do forgive . . . I do not like
To look back

I DO FEEL MAN'S PAIN AS THEY PLACE IT
On THEIR BAGS PACK

I like to erase, but not with Whiteout
I like to paint and see beautiful rainbows
If I can, I would grow love and water it . . .
I LIKE TO CAPTURE LIFE FOR WHAT IT IS
WITHOUT QUARRELS and no PERSIST

Love . . . IS A PASSION SEEN LOST AND THAN FOUND
Loves erase all hates . . . Erases all prejudices you should try it doesn't cost
A thing
Lives in all colors and welcomes all races
Love forgives all
And restores faith . . .
Love never dies . . .
Never ends . . .
True love no need to defend
For never bends . . .
It's an open language for all man to comprehend-
All man should stand
Applaud love it's the only language that doesn't go out of style
Is the only music all souls needs
Do not try to erase it with Whiteout

Erase Not With Whiteout

ERASE NOT WITH WHITEOUT

Erase not with your heart
Embrace your golden heart for its where love exists
and grows
I do not follow . . .
I do not lead
I am all silence
But for the Gods.

I am not a *plant*
I do need waters
I do need the *sun*

But most of all, I need love
To be *free* . . . To be at ease
I do bleed . . . I do not scar
I do forgive . . . I do not like to look back

I may not be black but I can feel their pains every
Time a white man turn their backs
I like to erase, but not with Whiteout
I like to paint and see beautiful rainbows
If I can, I would grow love and water it . . .
I would love to ask some folks why they don't like tainted skin or well
unspoken citizens
Why mistreat and make them a misfit so you can fit?
Why be so unfair and thus declare possible wars?

Love . . . Erases all
Lives in all colors and welcomes all races
Love forgives all and restores faith . . .
Love never dies . . . Never ends . . . True love no need to defend
For never bends . . . Doesn't it have a purple face?
It's an open language for all man to comprehend-
It a beautiful thing when love is on your hands and you passed it on to
other hands... take this baton regardless if not Field Day

Know that-
It's the only language all colored hearts understands . . . Love

All hearts is beautiful-
Pumps blood … it's a river that flows
Don't exit without feelings of love experienced it and keep it
Don't you ever lose this special keys that fits
All great man should know- love does grow
Know to lead takes a man with great dreams and strengths
To dream is not just a mindset but also a reality if you believe
Beliefs are within every mans' sleeves and reach
If we all want to seek peace . . .
We can all reach
Let's believe . . . seek peace love will always follow

All great leaders have one thing in common:
"They believe in nothing and everything with an open mind"
They believe in so much for mankind and are willing to die to save its
Kinds

They often stand alone at times prosecuted for their beliefs
That can reach the highest peaks in all with its depth . . . all matter of time
They believe in love for a higher Beings:
They dismiss what is not.
They welcome all colored rainbow

They take great pride paying the price as literatures states un-other wised
page filled
Sacrifice for love …Love is worth to die?
Loving totally . . . being known mortal you and I totality
All man and breathing things must always die except their great works
By which, gets better with times, as grapes of your finest wines . . .

The Winds of Time

Time . . .
What is it?
Men defined by time
Does time defines man?
Man is timed
Time are man...

Today's here
Yesterday's gone
Tomorrow's yet to come
Time clicking secondly in hurries
Why all the worries?
Whose feelings all the sorriest?

Who can tell the best of stories?
Why must man worry?
Who can build in a day?
I know only One claimed this glory
Today, He stands tall among all others...alone
He is indeed holding the Glories...of the finest, oh'yes

A gentle smile
Is all you might hear?
With the winds of time
As its witness
For sure does any one hear?
Is it all crystal clear?

The silent sounds
Of the babes gone by
Can you hear the silent cries?
Is nature screaming?
Why innocent babes must die?
I am on your sides

No matter what they may say or do...
Man are cruel but know it shouldn't be you
Seek to be all good despite what you see, hear, and revealed to you
Aim for a light
Walk away from darkness
Enter with love
Dismiss all that is not love... Accept God for He is the only TRUTH to
Love

Today . . . .

Today—"**I will change forever**"
My son 21 on Apr Fools' days, which flew as I unable to catch it
In Forever 21 shopped I, so recently-
As left years-youth behind
Now embrace his manhood of a beautiful man Of his be comings . . .
I shall leave all sadness behind
I shall move forward without looking back ever sad
I shall leave all behind
All doors shall open
All shut are behind
For he is on all my right sides
All my tears, He already dried
He's satisfied am benign
He witnessed lots
When I was lost, He found me
When I was depressed with no cures
I thought for sure, I die, oh no not I
He took my dirty hands and clean'em
When no umbrella onto my hands, He covered me blessedly
He even saw me perhaps more than confused
He saw me misunderstood as they took
He did see me, I might not be a dove but I could love
I was never tough nor was I ever weak
Oh' did He see me—"You're all Love in many ones"
How wronged they, "Maybe more than blind"
They mistook you more than disable
Unable to think, Oh no not
They took you more than a Silly Goose
You they thought a messy beautiful stupid of a goose
But as He stated, "Wait, not her"
We'll proof you wrong someday

You'll get up from your seat
One day you'll state—
"Where was she and came from?
She's been here all along invisible by man:
Spat and cursed
Left almost dead
Cried as none heard but I
Bled not running out of blood . . ."Gauzed by I
Wounded as no band aid could close the wounds . . . but I"
Breaking down in tears running down . . . Fearlessly?
Cracking down bones . . . Was all in the heads?
Seeking attention . . . Oh no, it's not her style . . .
Almost nailed like "J"—
But unlike I, a female carried by I'
Ran a NYC marathon with a pulled muscle
Proofed alright others wrong all the way to the finish line 4:38:03 in a
terrestrial rain

April 20, 2012, 8:30 AM

Yesterday . . .

Gone with winds-timed . . .
Yesterday gone
It shall never come
Today is the day to live
As yesterday is gone

It was not the wings that flew
It was not a ticking clock
It was not a flying saucer
It was not a machine

Gone was the concept of time . . .
It will never come back
Unless you dream like it
It will forever be gone as what was once was . . .

Times are of the essence
How many man let it go by
Never have I met a man
Who was able to catch it . . . it flew over the cuckoo nest

Lets be real . . . time doesn't stand still
It moves not with the winds
It moves not with your feet
It doesn't move never even with your precious insolence of the minds . . .

There's never a need to cry . . . and say why left without saying good-bye
It only this silence that is. What it is—"TIME"
Man goes to war . . . life cut so short
They go to sleep never awaken . . . did they catch it on their silence
Of man that now can't no longer sleep?

I challenge any man to bring back time
To bring it back wrapped
To curled in bed and state . . . "I am back"
This time well wrapped since was all trapped

Did the mind escaped
Did it come back?
Can it ever come back?
Did it ever found a home?—The question is, "Where is its home?"

Don't wait long
It be too late
Marvel at the skies—it's a paradise with lovely rides . . . colorable clouds
Of rainbows

Take a ride . . . Don't let time define you . . . be the definer
Preserve smiles with God
You will not crash—
He'll be by your side . . . when all else may divide
He'll sustain you and I . . . all intact inside swimming the deepest waters

A substance beyond all . . . rest on Him—He'll never complaint
Feeds on we. He'll never ask for much
Precious deeds He all this
You'll have many unfolding suns revolving. . . . Don't look back

He'll be your best tour guide . . . you'll see—
Just witness Love with Him or perhaps Her . . . Just believe
Takes His hands . . . take a deep silent walk
No longer alone as no speech heard . . . Silence of the lamb

Whispereth onto and awake today not yesterday not tomorrow leaving all
Your sorrows
See and learn most of all . . . the lovely of things
Wait long not yesterday is now . . . tomorrow not yet is today to plant
Tomorrow will bare fruits—fruit for those that planted

He gives lots . . . for a better tomorrow
So you can leave all your sorrows with yesterday
Today's' counts . . . so you can have all tomorrows
It'll be with Him-

Sorrows-winds taking it away
Suns carrying them afar
Meeting fast . . . you'll manage
One at a time . . . O'yes beautifully

Tomorrow

Tomorrow shall come
Today is the day to live
As yesterday is gone
As my mind wants to cry
I will not take for this ride
But preserve it with a smile with God

I shall not crash-
For God is on my side
When all else may divide
He'll sustain me
All intact inside
I shall swim the deepest waters

He's my substance-
I shall rest on Him
As He feeds me
I see all His precious deeds
As the suns revolves
I shall rise each morning without looking back

He'll be my guide
As I see-
He'll witness it with me
As He takes my hands
I shall walk with Him
No longer alone

As He whispereth onto me
As I awake-
He lets me see lovely things
I may not wait long
For He given me lots
Tomorrow, I shall be with Him

Sorrows-
May come
But the winds
Will carry them afar
As I shall manage
One at a time . . .

BELLS

As the bells ring the New Year
May it ring with love a new life to each heart.
As the sounding angels sing songs with a dove-
Lets's all rejoice and give hope for peace
May the New Year—
Enlighten each one of us with hope and more love
As we look forward
With plentiful love
May the season of love, hope and dreams—
Fill even lost hope that never exist
That can't be buried for peace exist
But can be found within our tender hearts
May the Christmastime—
Ring the bells of our beautiful hearts with more colorful love
Let us awake each morning with our guiding sun
Let's not lose hope and seek harmony deep within that is love

A Hidden Garden

All the hidden treasures are here . . .
Is where birds come to sing? Yes!

Is where there are colors waiting to be seen . . .
By your very naked eyes rainbowly

Is a paradise all in the skies . . .
As the waters falls paints a better picture than before

Now the blossoming colors all come to be . . .
Here, definitely where nature doesn't scream but beams

It's an oasis of splendor . . . In all 4 corners
Where every man should feel God's grandeur and splendor

A hidden star above all radiant . . .
A garden here below all hidden treasures

All angels are clasping
Singing of glory alleluias . . .

For sure for all man to hear . . .
So peace could exists all in here

Is where I want to give this literary gift to the world . . . Perhaps a little
bit of love
From the bottom of my pink hearts to theirs.

Hope you'll all enjoy these
Poetic and descriptive lines hold it and treasure."

HAIKUS (5, 7, 5)

NATURE HAIKU

Nature on its way
Waiting for the sun to come
All the flowers comes . . .

SEASON KAIKU

Fall, leaves do changes
Springs flowers, summers gets hot
In the winter gets cold

LOVE HAIKU

Love is an arrow
It strikes in the heart once
Leaves one almost blind

FAMILY HAIKU

A tree is a seed
For a family to exist
It's fingerprint is

MICROBE HAIKU

A microscopic—
To the naked eye, defined
Just waiting to hide

Death Back in Oct 1979

10/27/14 @ 1:30PM

I
It was an afternoon of September 1979
My youngest of brother's of initials- JEF
Met his near death-
As he rode his bike
I was told from Coney Island
There were traumas making all that didn't matter mattered
He is now near death in Bay Ridge ambulanced at LMC

I received a call-
It was from sister no.6 as were now almost 9
"**Y**our brother is almost dead
Wait for my husband to be picked up"!
I rushed to his side as I hurried and tried
Instead met him at 4AM almost dead
I then collapsed meeting this unfriendly floor as my friend…

II
The saddest of days came and rushed in...
An entrance of Fall-
I felt this fall... Something came knocking
Being of 19th in young years... focusing- concentrating in symbol of ∞
I know all of the lights just escaped, where did it go?

I do recall a college sophomore was all I
It was back in 1979-
Blinded from all sorts of agonizing pains
I sat sad quietly in my white bed matched by solid gold-trimmed of woods
I was full of pink panels and tiles all decorated by him

I could had preferred to pull all of my hairs
I could had screamed to awaken all of this universe
Those that are dead and/or undead-
Those in endless awakes and bodies lying with attitudes in solitude in the cemeteries
Those in extreme anesthesia for which in seconds I experienced amnesia

I was profoundly studying Calculus
I jumped from my seat
I approached the phone-
I experienced death on me and no tone and sent to a different time zone
I heard a refer of an unwelcomed death of a message I didn't prefer
I tried to exit death but, had no brain to comprehend reality

III

It was referred to my youngest of brothers
To send death to him even though he didn't deserve
He was in line number 4 and I #9
He was the one, I got along
He loved me discreetly...
He supported me completely
He was one- "Good things dies young!"

He respected all of me infinitely
He said... he loved me abundantly
He admired me as his favorite and Mari too
But, it was I-
Who made all his difference... He knew I was different

He sensed I was smart in all the areas
As I felt his death... oceans of hysteria followed me
Oh... No not I
No one could ever touch this area
I was there for everyone, even though none for me...
I've requested
I needed not seek anything at all
I just gave-
All of me...
Is who
I am

IV
I am-
Not one
To pretend
He always let me
Know this
For he always believed in me...
How unsaintly it was
That even with a tracheotomy... he was never the same
We all cried... seeing him in such states
To witness him like this
Death came to claim and proclaim his name
Oh.. No, it was more than clear of his un-dear wife who came and took
all the cake... she claimed it more
Did she ever love him are my vocabularies?
My mom and dad begging God

I could hear her pleads... Why my son is now gone?
I could see her tears running down the roads uncontrolled
I could sense her pains-
This is all insane!

I had to take a trip to ID his body-
It was to be exact Kings County Hospital of an afternoon again, oh why
life can be so vain?
I saw a huge glass door, as I felt it without any perfume
The curtains opened, a corpse I saw as was all he...
I indeed ID'ed this corpse, I became one with him
I became so numb all over me... I sliced my throat with pains and met
the floors; I'll never be the same...

V
I can't talk nor walk
An overwhelms of oceans of pains came running thru all of my veins
I experienced feelings of beyond un-calmness
What I've become is a body of corpse
I was a bit tan …Am I white now, I've no mirrors, can corpse see?
Look at me, I am frozen… My brother is now gone…he won't be coming
back!

I realized he's not here and/or there…
I am alone
But then again, am I?
I get no hugs from anyone
I am supposed to be strong for everyone
I know he is now gone… he who always made me feel as I were a very
special rose

I know you came to me
Way before you left me
You tried to let me know this
For sure that you love me so much…
You always knew… No one could love me as much… That you sent my
Jose just like your name as a replacement

Better yet-
You protected me from so much
Who could had foretold
That you were to be inscripted- not "**INRI**" but
It's "**That all good dies young!**"
I can only say why you had to die so young?

VI
You visited me-
To tell me how special I am
You so dearly made it all clear
I am the chosen one in this family
Not all matters
For is only love that does

You came twice in same week
In our home
In front of the house
As the traffic lights greened, even if I didn't scream
You serenely approached-
All from a distance

Instead your brown-green station wagon
It was crystal clear all for real in here-
It was white instead, and not red nor others...
It was a precognition as per my religion professor Dr. Lago
I now know... I am very special

Just knowing-
I had a super brother
That loved me
So very much...
The heavens are yours dear brother
For surely loving me so much...!

VII
You've departed
From this Blue Earth
On an Oct 22, 1979
It was the saddest and gloomiest of days as you were buried as time clocks
all stopped
This I can say your life gone and so ...
I followed you, for I was more than just sad...

Today-
Because of your beliefs in me
You've given me the wings to be...
I don't need visible wings
For I know
I've them- You provided it for me

I can claim-
Your name:
You were all love
For all your sisters
But, It was I, who
You always believed in...

VIII
As I placed a rose
Yes-
On your coffin
I took a ride with you and wanted to be buried with you
Then, why should I... This is not my time
I know, I will always be with you... I am riding on a white horse, you
watching over me

As your coffin was being brought down
To meet this unpleasant brown-stale Earth
The ground opened... the angels came and wept and so did I...
You didn't deserve to leave
Why did you have to meet your death...
Was this your time, I must ask dear Lord?

My Brother Came To Me From His Tomb

10/3/14 @ 8P #5 Train

Today of date Fri month of tenth on the 3ʳᵈ and century of 21 of year 14 (2014)

I dreamt of my brother of initials AAF-

Whom I buried Wed month of the eighth day of 6ᵗʰ in a heart felts...

As few raindrops showered upon us as well droppings of tears on my face surfaced

I felt the Earth resurfaced and the service of this wake as he awakes... to my dismay

Which love ones can take the many partakes of a man that 4days... does not awake?

It was the saddest of the days

As if all the suns of the sun was swollen all at once and I was left in darkness for a moment

Then again, as my mom quietly sat sad in row 1

As his dear wife and sister-in-law Presi calmed the water fall tears face in this area

I could hear his neighbor in hysteria-

As I know this dear Earth will miss him, perhaps in plenty of areas

Am I entitled to question the Superior one?
He who holds all the expertise in these areas and the keys that fits?
Why did the greatest of the Lord's
Carried him to his Gates of colored heavens?
For I do know, his heavens couldn't wait...
Like all good things comes to an end but, not for him...He now safe in
the clouds of the furthest heavens

In the purest of the heavens he is... I know is there, where he is
He belongs there, is where he is
Now looking down upon all we
Perhaps more real to believe... Is that he's looking on his beloved one's
He was so loved by everyone's
He did not wear the lucky number to be treated fair by everyone's ...
Who says life is fair?

I shall be getting back to this dream-
I so surely sat in row 1
I was solidly sitting without any winds and briefly with the presence of an
immense sun
I surely witnessed his rising like an elevator ride carrying him on to me...
I overcame an endless embrace of an amaze grace...
As he came to me, he sitting next to me, with arms well stretched over
and around me

He looked at me-
With such an increased immensity and density of an overwhelm tensely
He seemed so at peace as his presence was so at ease on me
Slowly swept away not by the breezes-
Entered back onto his coffin… and so his resting place…
This Earth once again closed, as was this brown mustard soil was with
him… Will I ever see him again?

Who can complaint? Why should I?
For chance was with me… that I dreamt with him… Oh, so recently
That I met him once again
This was indeed a dream
But it was really nice to see him again
He was indeed a man who tried to live his life as best as he could… I can
attest this over and over again

He loved his fellow man… his children and all
I have to ask and the maker of all the man and of the heavens-
Do I have to be more than good for this meet for an again?
I believe it's always the truth… as the desires' are there to express the
needs
Are my beliefs to be more than good to stand the test of times…
And not break nor tempt to break man's arm
I want the heavens to welcome me infinitely and others too, to no ends…
So now, we all have to advertise 2day.

A Waterfall Of Prayers
To All The Souls of Sept 11

You're all no strangers
I've been with you
Throughout the moments
I learned of your fates...
That indeed created by monsters

Memories of yesterdays, today, tomorrow is what we have
We've pay tribute to your lives...
In regards who can make this all alright?
Regardless times heals all wounds
But yours were to heavy a burden to close, where it has soaked up all gauze
So we're left with more tears as you've taken away many of our fears

We as a nation stood the test of times…
We all have cried
We all have felt your pains
We stood without handkerchiefs or napkins
But silently echoed prayers

Your names embedded and printed onto marble prints and now
matching these marble minds
We can still hear your screams you didn't deserve
We can get chills all again…
We can still remember innocents gone too soon
Mothers, fathers, sisters, brothers, aunts, uncles, niece, nephews, fireman,
policeman, clergyman and friends…

Why that life is never fair?
I dare any man to reverse this stately phase above
That life's pain that comes with life
But this one holds none
Was created by un-saintly men

We all know life carries an abundance of pains
When we were born-
I don't recall given a choice
I know we all born naked and our corpse exists
All the weights are love that holds it…

I pray for a world-
That tomorrow our children and its offsprings' can spring onto a peaceful
transition
Where all man can express their love for life
Where all negativity can be buried in the cemetery
Where only love can never be bury

I want all to witness the most beautiful prism:
In each corner of the galaxies viewing rainbows of hopes
Where all the sorrows are gone with all of yesterdays...
For it is today that counts, even though there's no hint of literacy
The only things that counts are all the pills for tomorrow, the pill of love

All man has to travel to one place
No matter where you are
We are all one
Seeking to be love...
Love is the greatest of all the bonds. Don't you ever break it!

"Man she learn to stop all what is not love
This may be tough-
But it tough to swollen a large pill
Even more the wrong one
Love is the only pill to swollen... Let be that."

My Friends Are . . . .

My friend is you . . . all anew
My friend is a new you as I try to forget thru trials
My friend is a new copy of a mirrored you being fruitful . . .
My friend is you unconditional . . .
My friend is a new you without a price since you've proven yourself
My friend is a beautiful person because I learned to forgive you
My friend is unique since we recognized is worth this try
My friend is this relationship that has passed and now reconciled . . .
My friend is not silent but all love for learned I will always defend
My friend I value for I know it been thru times we remained close friends
My friend is not an empty nest but a full treasure not of gold but of
hearts colored of red . . .
My friends are new experiences of times over and over again I will not
betray
My friends are moments whether we passed the times of hard weather or
not
My friends should know I can stand the test of times knowing we've
survived hard times . . .
My friend knows its thru crisis and even in or/not in good or bad, there I
am to defend-
My friend is I and those I will meet who can understand faith and
goodness always prevails
My friend is one who can complain and/or not but know I do have ears
that hears . . .
My friend may have had misunderstanding whom I am but then again
really knows who I am
My friend may be you and/or could be my purple heart I often dream
because at times I seem have none-
My friend is someone who can be silence, defend and stands by me for
believes in all of me
My friend won't deny me if really believes and honestly knows me

My friend and I have deep beliefs thru the nurturing years and
experiences
My friends knows that it has been thru memories that of being
immomerable always last and that you can look back-
My friend is someone who won't hurt because you can't put yourself first
and I can put you first if you're really my friend . . . .
My friend may be you
My friend may be anew
My friend is something new
My friend should be true
My friend may be He
My friend may be you
My friend I desire because its something new
My friend I treasure always whether permits and/or when feelings of
blues
My friend I stand whether the skies are blue or gray, don't matter
My friend I don't know where it is . . .
My friends, how many can we count . . . perhaps maybe one
Friends are priceless treasures; it's not an attachment or toy but a special
being
Friends truly are gifts from the above that beliefs are great white loves
Friends shouldn't cause hurts . . . its kind not vain
Friends are true love from the Divine
Friends are super man or woman . . . to your believes
Friends one ought to have provided even if is one
Friends when you find one . . . Treasure it for now you found one
Friends with one you may now never find yourself alone . . . since you
found one

Did you know that Cerveza-Microorganisms Spreading Holiday Cheer?

Cerveza Spanish-
It is beer… man's sports best of friends
A unicelllaur bacteria, a microbe, a bug-our ancestral line of life we owe
to all this
The formation of a life all link… we're multicellular-color derived species

Therefore, this holiday season, bottle opened-favorite wine shared
families/friends
Make toast to **Saccharomyces cerevisiae** ….

The "brewer's yeast" making wine and beer all what it is…
Did you know that-
Microorganisms Spreading Holiday Cheer
Yes, for sure…

A holiday season, bottle of favorite wine
Will warm hearts…

 Do toast to **Saccharomyces cerevisiae** a yeast
Know during X-Mas will be friend as you drink it wine and beer t/o the
nights

Ring the New Year…
Watch your favorite of games with Saccharo in your beer and wine on
your hands

An Angel entered heaven...August 10, 2016
And Ari is her name. "You will surely be missed."
- Minnie

Cause of death: Suicide

A *very special and artistic person* **Aracelis, a Graphic Designer**

R*eligious beyond comprehension and in multitudes of dimensions*

A*cquired immense love in her purple color heart as matched her favorite color*

C*aring for everyone with a love larger than anything I have known*

E*xquisite and well defined human being not hard to describe*

L*arger than life this silent person that everyone she knew she touched dearly*

I*ntelligent and soft as an angel was all* **Aracelis:** *she is in heaven with the angels*

S*inging songs of rosy alleluias the gate of heaven did opened...* **Ari** *is watching over us*

*There's no logic, as all laws have been broken, I recalled she made a beautiful
art out of a NYC token
She lived her life putting others first, at 38th of an age gone too soon... how
can we explain a broken spirit?
Her husband Stephen adorned her as all we... What went so wrong that no
one will ever know?
I only wished I knew and knew how to fix it... What have I not questioned,
have I given it all to Him?
I've prayed and always will that paths of lights not darkness are the answers
never suicide, seek help never too late, it's not a shame to be strong as you seek
to live!*

-Minerva A. Garcia, Auntie Minnie

Too young to die before he enter college Jonathan Hernandez, my cousin entered Heaven August 27, 2016

Cause of death: Drowning

A life gone too soon at tender age of 18th
He drowned Sat afternoon swimming across the Delaware River,
Barryville, PA
He was loved by everyone
A super human being at his young age

The search for his body continued til sat went down
Sunday 730 AM his lifeless body found without a life vest as
indeed a foolish act
His dad encouraged him to wear one
Listen, danger is out there!

You can't resist deep waters
Don't tempt your being a hero
You can't tempt fate nor ...
Police words, "While the water looks calm`, the current can pick
up underneath..."

He seemed to wear himself tired as he swam and gotten caught by
the currents underwater
His friend make it to shore seeking assistance
Listen if everybody's out their listening and you're out in water
—Danger
Depth are deceiving, water can be as much as 15 -20 feet deep
spots not foreseen
Wear a life vest anytime get in the river or water, states his dad-

Jose Hernandez is mourning the loss of his son
Anybody's out there listening water —Danger
Put on your life vest because, it will save you," Jose said.
Jonathan's cousin said, "He believes wearing-
A life vest in the Delaware River, should be the law."
What do you think?
Emphasis and suggestion great but common sense 100% better

Summertime's are times of proms and graduation like was for
Jonathan
Summer events
Vacations for fun and endless memories
Ready-in for college in the Fall, now these dreams were all gone
-Minerva A. Garcia

An Angel Entered Heaven petite and youthful April 28, 2017 named Rowena Garcia

She was a devoted wife, mother, daughter, sister, sister-in-law, aunt, cousin, friend, colleague, super nurse at Jersey Shore Medical Center and most of all a devotee catholic

Cause of death: head-to-head car collision

To the husband of Rowena, Geo *and Her children-Lauren, Julian and Jared*

May *all your salty tears like the salty sea be washed away through God's love*
May *you find the shores' and the shoulders' to rest upon by Him*
May *you wake each and every morning knowing He's near*
May *you always reach and seek His sacred name for He's love*

May *you never lose hope and question God's plan*
May *you always know you are guided and loved*
May *you be blanked by His tender touch and warmth*
May *you sense His presence and know you'll never alone*

May wish to know your mom is always there....
May you know she's an angel up above with beautiful wings
May you never worry that it's only the best He seeks to need
May you know that Rowena asleep but yet always watching over you she'll be...

Rowena carried on to the heavens as a car collision at 631 PM, Jackson, NJ
Fate she met on a tragic Friday evening, I recalled a call from my husband
at 1030 PM flat lined... I began to feel numb as my skull entered a feeling
a toothache and went blank unable to comprehend what was said to other
end... speechless

SAT afternoon a very special prayer and a good bye with my good eyes as I cried
Believing now the unbelievable she's gone, her husband and daughter victims too
I thank my Dear Lord as He spared both of them
He has His reasons for both of them...
-Minerva A. Garcia, Sister-in-law

Juan Herminio Nunez, my Brother-in-Law entered Heaven March 1, 2017

Cause of death: Carcinoma (Skin cancer)

To Carmen, Oscar, Carlos, Kristian and Rosie
Your husband … know that your dad was the greatest of guys…
He was funny as made so many laughed
His passion was his children and his jobs

He worked super hard to provide all for his kids
He loved his wife, my sister tenderly
I admired his charisma and joy for life, especially merengue

I never can recalled a day without his sunlight in til cancer stepped
in …robbing him
He always filled sunshine's…never giving up not even til the very
end
His laughter's was more than contagious

He had no enemies
If he did, he made it his friend…
He was unique because, he knew how to enjoy life and bring others
with him all in-fun

He fought a good fight with skin cancer for four years… carcinoma
was his only enemy
Memorial Sloan Kettering Cancer was his second home

With intravenous and machines as his second best friend as he and
all we thought
Cancer has no friends- it's a black whole and category 10 hurricane
I'll explain

At the end, who can fight the oncogenes? They are your un-best of
uncles'
There're not your uncles who can love and defend and comprehend
They're your enemies who has no friends…and no face

Even if your wear your favorite hats
Sometimes, may not be enough
Could be hereditary? All the why's that not even hats, sun tan
lotion nor the cloth on skin are not your friends… What can we do
to defend from this unfriend?

Just live your life best of all your cans
You only have today… be guided by love
Make it the best you can

-Minerva A. Garcia

Wilson Garcia
Battling colon cancer since 2016…
Today is June 12, 18 as I pray

Diagnosis (DX): Stage IV colon cancer
To Wilson's family, friends and his beloved mom, Carmen in
heaven

Saint Peregrine, saint of cancer, Peregrine Laziosi
Come to his aid
Why should he die?
Death the unfairness of it all…

Why chosen Wilson?
Is his mom so lonely?
Why you so needed?
Why take him?

He has no wife nor children
Shouldn't he experience love?
Why can You leave him with us?
Why you must take him from us?

He saw 1st fall of the WTC towers attempts, as escaped
He experienced and 911 covered in dust escaped?
With monsters in his heads of his colleagues and friends unable to
escape
Now with cancers as tumors running wild unable to escape

With intravenous tubes in his arms
Looking wasting away...as chemo treatments stays
For how long
Too many promises, with news you may only have days, months...
I am trying to negotiate with Him, my Dear Lord please I beg you
let him stay much longer

I don't know if He will listen to me
As I come more than a beggar
I love Wilson til death
I would cut my life short and all my veins if I can, so he can live
but I can't negotiate

Wilson, so sweet and angelic of a man... I say, life is not fair!
Why give a kind man a deadly dreadful news sentence?
Seeing my brother-in-law wasting away like his silence breaks my
hearts...I cry silently with the winds

-Minerva A. Garcia

Wilson Garcia, My Very special Brother-In-Law

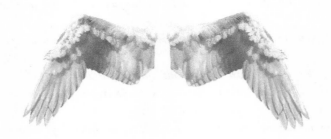

Willed and strong
Intelligent knowing history but in silence
Lovely as the softest bird
Special and unique in many ways
Often soft spoken as angels
No, extra special you are… You're an angel to me…

Garcia, you beautiful last name
Angel you always been
Rich in love as no other I known
Caring and loving you always…
Individualized brother-in-law full of love and compassion
Angel you really are… we all love you so much, know that.

-Minerva A. Garcia
6/4/18

My Dearest Brother-In-law

With an increased innocence of a white dove
Ill spirit never has
Love that doesn't exists in Planet Earth but Wilson's own
Spirit full beyond immense love
Owning very little seeking only to be loved
Never compliant, but only seeking to be loved

Gracious and profound love to match the blue skies
An appetite always for love
Regrets I can't observe much, only that which we can agree, "**Life's too short…**"
Capable only of immense love
In his heart only you'll find love
Acquaintances of love is all he has and I know peace in his heart he has always have

-Minerva A .Garcia 10/20/18

Tell Me Why

Please tell me why
Tell me all the whys
Why all the lies
Why your lines are never straight

Tell me if you dare
I am not scared
He who lives in me
He also stands with me

Tell me why you pretend
I know your intents
He who witnessed all
He always protects me

I have often question all of my greatest of the Lords
"Why you taken the entire good one are from me?"
But then I know, He has left the very few as a shadow only for me
Perhaps so I can believe more in Him… thank you Lord

Tell me why
I have felt so much pain
Tell me why
It can't erase for my mind are not an eraser nor white out but sponges of
living cells

Tell whys
As they say, "The good do die young?"
I also know
An once in their blood never had to be bad

Is this the ultimo sacrifice of goodness?
I can't ever be bad
Why you haven't taken me
I will always exchange, why not take me?

I can in a beat
But then again, is reserved for my husband that we one and my precious
son
As I pray for them and all my loved ones and all I pass thru life
My dear Lord, come for me whenever you've the need and sacrifice me
instead

But then again
You need me to endure
Do more of your work
That is left only for me

I shall always follow those commands
Perform the tasks
That only you can give
Knowing that I can complete

As you've placed all your faith in me…
As you know I can obey…
As you convey all to me
As I am your obedient disciple to follow thru..

There's are no denies here, I will always die for you
It is the ultimo price to pay for love that the very few will ever understand
and endure
As I will always stand by

As I been called upon to serve

Now is the time to understand all the whys
I do know, all the whys'
That by which must leave behind… not with an arrow nor with a sword
But with a torch of love to be shared

I've lived a life full of commitments
I've no regrets
I've embraced
Am with God's grace

If you ever begin to question
Why all this sacrifice
I can only say
There's no greater love than His

I have loved so much
I have stretched by my bones to be broken from neck-to-toes
Know was never my intentions
But man who owe me and did dare to break them

I fought battles in courts
From Strawberry store to Disneyland and I proved with my God together
we stand
Let no man divides this love found in our hearts
Know if any come between us, must answer only to Him who is stronger
than superman

You really want to know
Why I've sacrificed
Must you know?
I do know all the whys and why all the sacrifice... It's because, we stand
strong

It's not that we feed on each other
He feeds the fish, birds, and all we
Is that He only choses the strong
And always know are the weak that think are strong

I've never said, "I am strong"
It's been only He
Whose prove over and over again that I am?
Even I, have always question my strength

But then again, he response always the same...
"My Dear and Precious child
Why have you questioned all these whys?
When it's been always I

Oh, yes
I've forever fallen raindrops
Upon as white words fallen heavily
Super raindrops as you captured finely
Onto a naked white paper as you filled all by these prints

It's been only reserved for your
As your eyes thought to be blind
Oh, not you
A super mind that also shines.. Oceans of discoveries are all you

Let it be know
Wisdom of beyond matureness
Strength with incredible endurance
Makeup of a Goddess… not so difficult to understand

A name to match the Astros
Then again, true
Minerva, Roman Goddess and Greek Athena God of wisdom
Borne all Saint's Day

All not by chance
It is I that rules, not man
I stand tall and high that only the most privileged can see me
As I've chosen you as one… No memberships are required but love

Let it be known
Men do divide
But you are not one
You don't follow… nor lead, as you always sought to be next to me

Let it be the end
Let it be the beginning
Let it be vice-versa
You can never be convicted of a crime you didn't commit… As I witness,
always I'll be

-Minerva A. Garcia,   SAT 10/20/18 720AM near VNB by Hylan
BLVD Staten Island, NY (Stopped car to write)

They Say Am Crazy

Torn apart ... aches in my hearts
My heart feels
As hears such hurts
"Stone may break my bones, words will never hurt"; it's a lie, because it's
all hurts

To aim to be
To desire only to be
To work at it... one day at a time
To reach a goal, that is... to be only at peace... perhaps not so perfectly
but just try to be

Knowingly you are human
You can reach to be
Know you can't ever be superman and/or superwoman
But you can always be the better person to master change

Aiming to be
Not trying to be others
Just only be myself
For all eternity...with my bodily castle

If you say am crazy
Why you think I am?
I know am not
Is all the matter that matters? Yes.. Y..e...a....a....a...a.   ..
Y..e...a....a....a...a.

They say am crazy
They say I am crazy
For all I've is love
I believe in love

They say am crazy
Because all I've is love
I've a plant only loves to grows
I water it abundantly, only love grows

I've a home
Where only love lives
You all welcome
You can always visit me

My only house built with love
The strongest foundation of all
You can find this material in my inner hearts
You will never find stones nor bricks

They say am crazy
They say I am crazy
Because you can only find love… I don't care if they say I am… don't
matter to me
Love the strongest of all the bonds… It's where you can always find me, if
you ever need to find me, it's where I'll be

Minerva A. Garcia SAT 10/20/18 740AM near Old Pfizer building
Brooklyn (Stopped car to write)

An untitled of LOVE
Commitments of Love… A gift of Love
Treasures of Love… Oh I 'How I loved… Decide
your title?

Thanks to those who truly hated me… I will never know why… I know, all I given is love
I don't know anything else, but love … Sorry, if it's all I have ever known
I've my reasons, "I have said- "**Thank U**"- As you know, too much…
Perhaps **1000's X's**
Know more, I had a great mom, Carmen; who taught me only to LOVE

Please excuse my paraphrase,
Know if you hated me or didn't like me
You made me strong…
Thanks to those who dearly loves me… I know it in all of my hearts being a work of art

It's been thru all these years that my hearts grown extremely strong as my body grows weaker
I know those who've cared … and those who have not… It's all ok
Know, I love same… as my heart is for all
No matter what… you all important to me

As I speak from my heart… no lies here, I give my faith and devotion as I pray to My God
I will not forget each and every one of you
I will always love you in full abundance
Because is what I've always known…

Please excuse me, if my words may hurt even the very least
I never meant too… I just want you to grow your heart with love taller than the highest sky scrapers
To those who have blessed, loved, nurtured and cared for me… I can't never thank you enough
Of all the blessings I've ever received and know… know that is love since always will last

If I ever have to look back, I would say and have said, "**Life is just too short**"
Therefore, do all you can today, since you know 2day, yesterday winds took' em
2mow the world's is yet to know…
How interesting, X-mas day borne

My favorites of holidays:
Halloween, Thanks Giving and B-Date
Am I that especial borne on our Savior date?
I shall let it up to you to be that of the greatest of a judge!

To those who've indeed allowed me to entered your blessed life....
I thank you in an abundance, as I preserve all of it, it's been a gift I'll treasure all of it
For me, I don't want you to ever cry... All I want is you to love and plant many of it
Get a plant if you don't have one... Please don't you ever 4get to water it

If I can once again, go back
All I can only think
I would only give more love
Since is the only thing that will always last

Whenever you want to remember me
Always know
Was only love
My heart has ever known and grown... and if I've ever offended you, 4give me, I never claim to be perfect

I may have never taken a vacation
I may have never own much
I may had work an abundance
Know, was love I placed no efforts... just flows like a river, learn this much is not much

If you ever begin to question this writer
Why she's written for me...
Don't slap her
Instead slap me... in the back while I sleep

Writers and Poets expresses... writes freely without rewards, but perhaps
if it could be viewed for the few
Why? - Because
Whomever wants to grasp
You may not have to be a magnet nor superman, know that

Today, am whom am
I have seen those here and those who've left
All I know 2day... we are not infinite, neither are all those things
Nothing will ever last 4ever... always know that... hope you all learn to
love, is what last

I've so much to thank
Yes... especially those who've stay
I want 2thank you 4that
Don't u ever cry 4me..

I will 4ever be in a better place
I know my best of Mother's next to me
I know more than that... She's in Heaven just waiting for me
I will 4ever be happy 4this meet... and well taken care, I know; will 4ever
be

To all my friends... Families and all
I've grown more than 50 ft. tall
Despite my frail body doesn't show
Know it's always been my heart that grows that the very few of man have
seen
If you've ever heard and/or listened
I've said not much, but thank you a billion folds
Know that I only been mastered only by love
Know more, 2day I am worst so much more, because I've always valued
"What is LOVE", don't ever4get that!

-Minerva A. Garcia, Sister-in-law   10/24/18 @ 2PM

My Dearest Brother-in-law... How Special you

With an increased innocence of a white dove
Ill spirit never had...
Love that doesn't exists in Planet Earth but
        Wilson's own unlike no other known
Spirit full beyond immense love as we"ll never know
Owning very little seeking only to be loved as we know
Never compliant, but only seeking to be loved as we know

Gracious and profound love to match the blue skies we know
An appetite always for love, we know... sacrificed all 4love
Regrets I didn't observed much, only that which we can agree,
        *As he states-"**Life's too short...**"*
Capable only of immense love... and more as it grew
In his heart only you'll found love and more love...
Acquaintances of love is all he had and I know peace in
                his heart he has always had
Wil was all love... All he wishes are, peace as he leaves gifts 2 siblings

-Minerva A .Garcia, Sister-in- law 10/26/18 @ 530PM

I took You To Heaven… To meet Your Mom

It was on Wednesday of a 24th
Of a year 2018… of an October month
It took me 10 minutes
For a powerful poem all of you…

O'how, I knew
Your day was Fridayeth all coming to soon
Of an afternoon that… I knew
Would come oh-so too soon… as your life ended

I, ended this poem at 210PM
It was indeed still this afternoon
I, released by my boss-
I shall not name to protect not from HIPPA but sounds likes D…

A visited to our EHS
A clearance mandated for all Health Care Workers
A FLU Vaccine- as a copy of this vaccine proof a congeal employee exist
Before I managed to be called, a call from my hubby

It was 220PM I might say
"My brother just died"
I walked out the door
I got near the elevator

I took a large breathe, may not enough
I know it was Wilson's last
Just few minutes ago...
He's now with his mom next to her and so she by him... all lovely to me
for this meet

Wednesday night, I dreamt
I was besides his bed at Calvary, Bronx
As he called out to me...
Can we talk a bit... I felt his silence

He tells me-
"Minnie, come with me... since he never wanted to die alone"
I wasn't scared at all
I felt loved with his innocent smile and courageous fight on this
oncogenic war ravaging thru...

I saw him collapsed onto my arms
I felt him wanting me to take his hands and hand him to his mom
I saw the bluest of the skies
I carrying him up so high...

Only I can sense are those lights not so hard to describe
As if mountains always there, and now barely see' em, knowing your eyes
capturing them
There they are, an invisible clear bluest of them all lights...
Am immensity all beyond all realm
It's a reality not so hard to describe

As I approach… as we reach these lights
We become one and as two angels wings invisibilities
I saw his mom just waiting for him to come
He also waiting nicely for this meet… I introduce

I see from a distance… not too afar
His mom waiting by this immense invisible gate as the blue light pays a guide
I saw a smile and so endearing
Her see her lovely tender smile

I knew this meet would come
He waiting this long for it to come
I was relieve more than a bit
Now forever together they'll be mother and son

I saw her smile
I saw her face
Mother Thrice Admirable
Mom, Wilson and then I hand over their son's a glistening of the eternal sun

-Minerva A. Garcia
11/20/18 at 625 PM

My Blood Is Not White

What colors are the bloods?
You all may say is Red
You may think is black
You may say, let's open all man

There's are no debate
You may cut all man open
All man same image
All man created equal?

I say, we are not
Explain why we not all same class
Explain why born perfect body
A child borne imperfect mother's habit of a drug

There's always a price
Why the innocent must pay
Why a man paying a crime didn't commit
Shall we blame society as he pays for their sins?

I say, we should all be in trial
Let the first without sins cast the first stones
No one wants to take the blame
Every one wants to live free by enslaving the innocent man

Once again I shall ask
What are the colors of our veins?
I say is not red
I say are the color of every man face

Because is where the true man can free express oneself
Everyone has a face
Despite its color
It can feel pain

I know I am not a fool
I know one as I see one
But, who am I to judge
I leave all the Great Divine

I can place it on the beauty of the strongest
Being of that of a Supreme
He is the only Super being neither you nor me
But I do know He loves you and me and also I, are my greatest of all of
my beliefs

If you ever find yourself lost
Seek only Him
Place all your faith in Him
He will take you to places, you never been putting you to the most
comfortable of sleep

Learn with grace
Master His inner being
Live with Him in Him
Honor all of Him

Believe He lives in your heart and mind
Doesn't matter if other question your insanity?
Know He can put you to sleep when all medicine fail
He can direct you to the best MD whenever He needs rest

Know more
You can color your blood to match your moods
As man withdraw your blood, red will not
It'll be the color of love to match his golden heart that is all art

If any man ever question this love
All you need to say
You've found the great art
You can only find it in the only one of a man traveled Earth that man was
unable to understand

If you ever call and place on a trial to defend this love
He may never be a witness but you can defend love with your heart's action
He stands always alone like a distance star
Is there you will find Him at night and day riding on the clouds... seek
Him, His face he can paint

Know if you heart are in pieces, He can put them all together
He can re-paint in your blood from red to white and reverse
As is all white, He put 'em back ...He is a master piece who can
Paint all as you un-like, know it can be black and/or any color

Minerva A. Garcia
SAT 10/20/18 715AM near VNB by Hylan BLVD Staten Island, NY
(Stopped car to write)

How Do I begin to Describe?

To describe requires a descriptive mind
It requires energy of the senses
To find the images whether real and/or fantasies
To be able to go the distance as distinguish the difference

I always prefer to go the distance
To seek the reality to all of my beliefs
An existence in the presence…To know today
To foresee the future as I work at timely… secondly, hourly, daily,
weekly, monthly and yearly

To know my Dear Lord,
To the distance you want me to go all the way
It is for you I must go thru
It's you I see at this distance

It's for you I run the furthest
It's why you placed all your faith in me
I now must put all to rest
You've proven over and over again, together there's nothing we can't
accomplish You and I

Perhaps believed by some, oh no too many
I am the weakest of all the links
You prove over and over gain
It's the opposite, of those whom may believe

As it doesn't matter
All that matters
All my blood is same as all
I do bleed but it's only You that can provide the absorbent to heal my
deep wounds

You've always come to me in all my needs
You've put me to sleep
You've listened to me
You've given me all I sought

You've understood all of me
You never abandon me
You've always stay with me
You only have understood me

What is that you haven't given me?
What is you haven't listen?
What is that pain you haven't understood?
Who is that person you haven't punished, teaching them a lesson?

I know you always come for me
I know where I can always place all my of faith
I know we ONE... doesn't matters if is questioned
As my faith grows, a microscopic seed of the most beautiful flower as is...
will always be

Minerva A. Garcia
SAT 10/20/18 720AM near VNB by Hylan BLVD Staten Island, NY
(Stopped car to write)

MY mother given all to me

There's no words to describe my mom, but a bright sun,
She is this beauty all within of innocence
That nature can only see... why she still like this at 97

She of the most beautiful of melodies... now I understand
She can sing with the birds ... loving all her plants like me
She super sweet and kind and gets better each years like you're finest of wines
My mom is really one of a kind and all mine. I thank God for this?

A mother casts her dreams into the sea .... for her offsprings
Hopes of all kinds ... With loveliest of eyes infinitely like the skies
My mom is all mine to love but she gives more always
I am super proud God choice, for my mom

Today, I like to honor you abundantly
I know I will forever be cradled in your arms of love
I also know there's never be a stronger love
I know I can always run for your love

You mom are my rock, my nest and all as you love me
I've so many beautiful memories because of you
All I've have I owe to you, mom
How can I ever thank you, mom

It's your day today, may God always continue to bless you
Know I am bless to have you as my mom…. You like no other mom.. So
unique like a dove…
All full of love… I love you mom …On this Mother's Day Mom, I want to
say "I love you endless".

Please know, that it's my heart that speaks all of this, you so well deserve to
know this!

Happy Mother's Day
To the most beautiful
Mom the world needs to know- "You're my star mom and my rock

Women Uniqueness Borne For

(A dedication to World Women Day (WWD) 3-8-2019

Part I
Women are born
For greatness
For mothering
For nurturing
For leadership

Women are born
For bearing children
For knowing the difference
For loving beyond
For continuing the human race

Women are born
For worshipping herself because beliefs with the Almighty to predict we are love
For only women has the beauty within uniqueness to feminists
For only women puts on makeup to beautify her own uniqueness
For only women wears a skirt because she prefers one to match her unique physique

Women are born
For making man strong by giving birth to men
For giving an abundance of the self-endless love
For creating a mirror image of the Women's' Movement with all her
brainy moves/impeccably cool
For liberating herself because she own it... Make room, a strong woman
just entered the room

Women are born
For creating masterpieces of impressions
For awakes for the best of man, the sun
For asleep by the nicest star, the moon
For shines unlike nor any stars, for she's a star

Women are born
For inner strength
For endurable passion
For lasting genes, to wear nice jeans and spray pink with it... using
lipstick if not fruits
For everlasting love as its fingerprints for all generations to see and be
fruitful only God approves

Women are born
For are indeed borne
For I say, not to follow a man
For I know, are man that follows
For, do not lead nor follow, I only commend, "What about you?" Define
yourself as you elevate

Women are born
For to be...
For to be its own
For to be loved
For not to be taken as slave not treated like one

Women are born
For to be more than equals
For they required all man to stand
For they thus earn your respect
For only a woman can lead a man to be a man... through birth also
touched by man

Women are born
For leading man to be
For she becomes free
For she frees man
For man must learn to be free... she' free

Part II
Women are born
For there's no doubt
For there's no escape
For there's no misconception
For women are the creatures for man to exist like any man should...

Women are born
For incomprehensible strengths
For inner unconceivable powers being mightier than any man
For she weeps not because she's weak
For she's stronger than any man, perhaps more than Superman: "Did he ever never exist?"

Women are born
For strengths come from far within
For with such in-durable passion
For she never gives up
For she stands tall despite 4 feet tall

Women are born
For she has incredible might's
For she may show slowness at times
For she doesn't fail time
For she always gets up

Women are born
For even being knock down
For even more downed, knocked up
For greater yet, left for dead
For no greater strengths endures any man

Women are born
For she man not resemble exact as man
For she must be taken serious
For I say should
For, not because fragility, but for the love of man

Women are born
For woman should earn her respect
For woman must earn her place
For woman must never degrade
For woman are the greatest strengths and the best possession any art can
be written

Women are born
For are **We**
For are **Must**
For are **Not trash**
For are **ourselves**, we are all "**ONE**" strong

Women are born
For with incredible light
For with it, light the world
For with our uniqueness
For with full capacity to embrace all with love

Women are born
For with incredible might with God's compassion
For with trust from the Divine
For with distinction to honor man
For with a kiss and a soft touch, she can transcend war to peace

Part III
Women are born
For opposite image of a man
For uniqueness all her own
For possesses qualities of delicacies as every month she's unlike men
For she may stained red but unable to write it only the DNA's all links
understands this red ink

Women are born
For she may feel comfortable on her favorite jeans
For its her DNA's along with all its uterus as its expands
For she can give birth
For witnessed uneven 9

Women are born
For giving births to man
For never giving up
For leading man to be…
For she can open the door nicely without making a sound

Women are born
For seeing great lights as few see
For is the way should be…
For the guidance of a river
For thirst to lead that waters to gives and sees as the colored rainbow gives
birth as man witnessed

Women are born
For giving births to great men
For breastfeeding this incapable creature(s)
For bringing to life what once was none
For now letting the world share a view and give proof she's indeed a
woman borne to lead…

Women are born
For all should step to the side
For all should let her in
For all she bowl to her
For she's unique unlike any other creatures

Women are born
For never giving up
For capturing a babe's cry
For listening to the universe cries
For giving all she has-dying for her borne child… taking her cloths flesh
dried becoming 1 universally

Women are born
For she may not complaint
For she may not have much
For she may sacrificed all
For she only believes in love, the most costly of all possessions man will
ever have

Women are born
For she may be in the darkness
For she knows how to come out
For she must rise like the sun
For her strengths does meet

Women are born
For are now coming out of the darkness
For perhaps placed purposely by some
For she now knows how to remove it
For she's become fearless… "Dare any man prove me wrong?"

Part IV
Women are born
For standing out of the darkness
For commanding her bravery
For fighting for peace and the love of man
For now she learned to fight for herself

Women are born
For increased love
For an extension
For what ought to be…
For now comes the time to stand hand-in-hand to fight for this great
Earth that is not a man

Women are born
For there's trillions of stars
For there we see the most beautiful of lilies
For there remains an undiscovered flower never seen by man
For there's lies a silent woman crying for the sins of man

Women are born
For she may not appear clean but dirty with a rag
For she may be homeless and confused
For she may be broken trillions of pieces
For I can bet you, she has always cried in silence

Women are born
For I can tell you
For I know whom been watching
For I will never know all the whys, neither will you
For the sake of God, "Does it matter?"

Women are born
For coming out of the darkness
For now being in the light
For she holds an invisible torch
For she leads the world toward the light

Women are born
For she's opposite image of man
For she has uniqueness unlike man
For she strive to be
For she lets man see and be.... As all man should

Women are born
For bringing out the light
For standing by all rights
For removing the stains
For darkness path of man

Women are born
For diffusing and erasing hate
For protecting the creatures that never came to be
For caring for her fellow man
For believing one day, she'll be free

Women are born
For not accepting the court's decision
For fighting for peace
For turning lies into strengths
For never giving up despite no strength left to fight

Part V
Women are born
For being buried and forgotten by some man
For they deliberately treated her as not her own
For thinking a different species perhaps
For learned to prove there'll never be a creature as a woman created by
this invisible man

Women are born
For fought the courts
For fought the laws
For fought the masterful
For fought those who thought never her to be... no fools she, a woman
borne to be

Women are born
For she flew without wings
For she was given bountiful gifts
For she escaped beautifully
For she had friends with the God's not by man

Women are born
For she's not a goddess
For she's not superwoman
For she's not a serpent
For she's just a woman wanting always to be free… today's she is

Women are born
For she knows
For continuation of life's we all be
For beyondness of our existences 46 chromo's be…
For the endurance of all to be.. survival of our uniqueness to be

Women are born
For keeping this contract
For this unbreakable bond
For is what we all have
For is that we all are we… one unit of a tree of our inheritance twine and
intertwine genetically

Women are born
For which man can dispute me?
For I may know approach with such intellect
For I may seem as a crawling creature with human existence thought by
the few
For proving all wrong is a task I get it from the Gods

Women are born
For The Supreme
For The Beings
For That of All
For Thus came to me...from the unicelluarity a cell came to be... thus
are all WE

Women are born
For BELIEVING IN LIGHTNESS
For BRINGING TO LIGHTNESS
For BELIEVING IN THE LIGHTS
For LOOKING UP ABOVE DAYS AND NIGHTS

Part VI
Women are born
For KEEP A CONTRACT WITH GOD
For KEEPING THIS MASTER CONTENT
For NOT MAKING HIM UPSET
For EMBRACING HIS STRENGTHS AND ACCEPTING OUT
WEAKNESS

Women are born
For OBEYING HIS COMMANDS
For DELIVERING MAN A SON
For LOVING HIS UNIQUE HANDS
For SHARING HIS LOVE HUMANELY

Women are born
For Ruling with increased strengths
For never having to say- "I do give up!"
For putting man to the test
For never resting til all sons become men

Women are born
For standing the test of time
For providing with breads to live
For working beyond dawn… not because a hobby but because …
For not crying as the spine becomes numb with unbearable pains

Women are born
For begging man to stop as she bleeds red blood not black
For all man bleeds the same red blood
For there's no inequality
For all man sheds red blood

Women are born
For never complaining
For she's proved made of love not steel
For not sleeping enough
For staying up with her infant son

Women are born
For knowing the difference
For she knows child borne always no matter what out of her love
For keeping safe for the sake of peace
For not letting man steal peace she'll fight to never be there's an end…

Women are born
For knowing she lives 2defend the innocence
For knowing it's up to her
For knows how 2increase love for peace to exist
For knows when to die 4peace in order 4all2be

Women are born
For sisterly love
For sharing love
For never giving up on love in order to increase more of it…
For sacrificing all of it…only 4love to exists

Women are born
For understands love
For giving love
For obeying love
For mastering love

Women are born
For sustaining love
For giving more love
For never abandoning what is love
For defending only what is love

Women are born
For describing love
For letting go what's not love
For complying/living the rules of love
For never letting pure art of love

Women are born
For the greatest of love FOR LOVE"
For loviest of KEEPING LOVE
For PROVING SHE'S LOVE
For LIVING 2BE LOVED AND LOVE

-Minerva A. Garcia 3/8/19 559PM

Crystal Pouring Letters of Love to My Sweetheart As & Has Rained

It's been so long-
Where did all the years go?
Where did all our love go?
Did someone captured it?
My Dear Lord you who always come to me- It's now that I seek

Where did I go? Was my Sweetheart always with?
Did someone steal me from him? I must know
Who had me hidden?
Who let me go or out, who helped me escaped?
Was my love that strong that I allowed myself to set myself free...

You're my un-colored bettlebug
I've always called for you in my unasleep
You've always managed to put me to sleep
When brightest of colors washed away by the silence of the seas

You've always rescued me from the un-aslee..eep
You've put me in a deep sleep
Every time I've called for you
Do I thank you and/or Do I admire you?

You've understood all of me
I've never questioned you
Why should I need too…
You've been the greatest of all of my friends

You've taken my hands
You've set a blanket in my sleep
You've set a special bed just for me
An a leaf as my blanket and ocean as my bed as the silent winds gently
put to sleep

You've calm the bravest of all the storms
You've found a noted bond we both can agree upon
You've let me go…
You held me tight and so… I won't fall

You been seen as a tiny creature
With colors of dark orange and tints of black and few dots
But never have I…
I've only seen you as my dearest of all of my friends

You been so unique to me
Why do I state?
Because in all of my sincerest of the states
It's you who always managed to put me to sleep

Sleep is just as important as food
Is the sunlight of the mind?
Is the moon yet all in a honeymoons
It a meet you now have found to keep…

You've rest a plant, a flower as your bed… as you've appreciated God's
Earth
You may have jumped from flower-plant to capture a moment best most
fit
You've touched my live as no human have … and so it is that you've
paced me to sleep
A blanket in the calmest of seas, you've allowed me to see and just it "I",
who become all free, am all me

Minerva A. Garcia 3/22/19 @ 320PM

I came to the river to find me
No, but for a very special task

I came to the river ...
To take away the thirst from my siblings

I came to the river with a purpose ...
I will never left, unless I completed all of my tasks

I came to the river ...
In the river, I discovered a mirror-image of all me

I came to the river ...
With an innocent mind ...and always did til this day

I came to the river ...
With two aluminum barrels, string attached to it and safely mantled on
my donkey

I came to the river ...
With a friend... I don't recalled its name, but I always knew it was a
friend I sat on

I came to the river …
This four legged un-maned always carried me to this river in DR

I came to the river …
I know, it was only once we both fell to the ground, I trapped with my tiny legs underneath

I came to the river …
With the obligation and responsibility I must give my family clean water … and so they can eat

I came to the river … and in the river almost drown
No matter what, I always delivered fresh water to siblings who now I know seemed asleep

Minerva A. Garcia 3/22/19 @ 325PM

The very moment I held
My life change... 4ever
Until this day... I know still changing 4me 4better
I know you changed me, to aim higher ... I done 4all us

All of yesterdays, todays and tomorrows' growth of more love
I loved, cared, supported, and protected beyond-never letting go...
despite a grown man
Am proud of the man you've become and always will be...
The moments I saw you take off with 1st steps, bicycle, school, dating...
moving on, all ok

I will always miss these vital steps
But know, always never far am
In the sun and/or in the rain
In the summer and/or in the winter

I've nowhere to go...
I will always have a home
You will always have one too
But together, always one for "LOVE"

I've raised you
I've let you go
I've treasured you
I've missed you so very much, you'll never know… all ok, I do know

A son's
Sunshine
Offspring of mine
No one can ever take you away from me, since God brought you to me

-Adda (Mom) 3/22/19 550 PM

I am not a bird, I can still question, who came for me? Was it because my beliefs took to be free
Know it is I who speaks of nature with all of its liberties that's me...
Come let's all breath free
Let's all accompany nature carefully nurturing and set it free
Let's no let hurt one another in the name of freedom and the statue of
Liberty for doesn't speak

I can now once again come back too seek more... am not one who easily gives up
Did you really get that!
I will protect my family my Jose and my My Sir James, my Knight
I say, was it you with all the love
That my pink hearts has been shown to me, its really a work of art

Was it you?
Yes, was you my love!
With your new smell of perfume
Once again, who have come for me
Was it you who've rescued me

Who was that broke all of me even my pink colored heart? And why?
It was you and only you alive I can trust, all good for me... know that my
Sweetheart
Who can ever questioned our love
There's no doubt it's Divine, I've taken no wine
Believe me, are the reasons many envy us as tryst to hurts me... been so
many of my burdens carried

I want to let you know I've died for you and returned ...that how strong my bond of love is for you
Its crystal words of Love I see and capture
I see and feel it as my breath speaks free
It is I who feels and breathe free for you
You'll always be my Sweet art, Sweetheart and more...for hear now and forever more...Amen

Know, how our love has grown
With James, Spaniards Patrick of Spain as we fooled
A very nice deal
April Fools' Day borne
With Danny Song's we all became 3, still 30 years married and approaching 36 years known of dating

Your love, wife
Min... Min... Min, known as Minnie
But better yet known as Minerva A. Garcia well known declare at times
Minerva A. Frias-Garcia
Minerva Frias my youth as 2/10/16 @ 320PM my pen marked my feelings
Printed as being more than just strong, infinite Love Bond to all the worlds and Lovers... This passion alive who have survived all the tornadoes, storms, illnesses, weakness, pains and takes all ways buried deeper beyond the deepest of the seas, now enjoys all of life's pleasures with my sweetheart arms...

-Minerva A. Garcia 2/11/16 425PM
Cell: (646) 284-7891

It's Not A Song But Just A Talk Of Bang, Bang Bang Lyrics To Me

Part 1

I went to the bank, TD by Central Station—
Reported a bang that happened to me feelings of abrasions
It was a cell call bang a $100 gift claiming $$$ from me
She requested my acct number
A charge of $3.91 . . . bang
A thief she turned out to be . . . with a bang, I reported this unknown ass
perhaps made of brass
An investigation proved I was right . . . Was she full of gas? Bang

Part 2

To ensure she doesn't steal from anyone
I bang her once, twice so she can be history . . . for everyone
This was a scam but I bang her so there'll be no more histories of her for once
As X-mas nears she could had bang tons of people . . .
Perhaps she did, but it was I who wanted to put a stop for no more reacts
Bang, bang, bang . . . hope they've put a stop
I couldn't stop the hours not of times . . . I wish I had an hour glass to beat
her with it

Part 3
I am tough?
I once was
Until too many bad things happened not by choice nor will
None were my faults . . . I say, "life is not fair!"
But I strived with it all as:
Bang, bang, bang
I thought I would die

Part 4
But oh'no, not I, I've survived
I entered with a bang, bang and bang
Leaving so many behind-
I got slapped in the train by a homeless man
I got rescued in Central Park by a homeless man
As I wrote a poem of him titled-
In the Park , bang, bang, bang!

Part 5
I buried my brothers: 1979, '07 and 2014; and my dad 2011
My precious mother-in-law 1999, I do hope to see no more . . .
I were told '94 I cheating? All, while sat quietly in row 1
How could I . . . as my professor sitting in front of me
It's a poem I write, am never a cheat! I've high regards
Today, to prove all these prints should serve once hiding/feeding me!
How distasteful, it left me anorexic to all of these of an un-believes

Part 6
I got so sick . . . as my supervisor threaten me, was she more than sick??? Just ask me!
Accusing me, I force staff to literate+lines on me an opposite to her discrete
I tended to delete her voice speech
Perhaps wanting to let her not speak
But this is not me despite her willingness to deliberately strike me
It seemed as if took all the bullets aiming at me, I wouldn't die . . . bang
For sure its not my time, bang that, this time!

Part 7
Trying hard to kill me . . .
Bang unable to succeed . . .
Death can't come to me
Not my time, since you've no right over me . . .
Bang, bang . . . bang that
U may want to divide-
Having no substance for life?

Part 8
Removing/Touching my work Vitek's cards
With her dirty hands
Now trying to write me up
Instead I wrote poems framed them
Framed/posted on hospital's lobby
Requested by the CEO, bang that
Can you hurt me more?

Part 9
I will always strive . . .
I stand to be a success
Despite ur ugly intentions
To scar—
Skin alive
Does bothered me?
What to think of all this?

Part 10
Recalling your scheduled 2-10P
Always in the lab—24/7
You had the bugs
How sad?
Forced out from your wills, a bad seed you turned out to be . . .
You didn't belong there . . . you got what you deserved, bang
Am I bad . . . No, never, get that bang!!!

Part 11
A Horticulture class in HS
With my own tree maps
Herbal medicine gathering all the leaves
Writings of a perfect paper
An assignment I responded well
With its phylum and class, genus
And its species to be exact

Part 12
A Willow tree or Maple tree
Willow
Kingdom: Plantae
Phyllum:Tracheophyta
Class: Maqnoliopsida
Order: Salicales
Family: Salicaceae of Genus: Salix with its Species: Salix

Part 13
Maple
Family: Aceraceae
Classification: Angiosperm
Phylogeny group: Sapindaceae
Species: Acer pesudoplatanus
How many species: 128
Where: Asia, USA, Europe, northern Africa

Part 14
Medicinals of Maple tree at the sap:
Benefits for your souls you might not know
A natural sugar for diabetes
Its syrup with its polyphenols/phyrohormones
Nurtures the pancreas making insulin's if you didn't know
With its zinc aiding the healing process . . . benefits with prostates
There's more lowers the rate of atherosclerosis as prevents oxidized fats/
cholesterol

Part 15
With class and its phylum all complete
The teacher came to me-
I handed my paper filled pages
With his states not in the right frame of mind-
"Would u come to diner with me?"
An excursion of "No" I left it at that . . . bang that
His response, "I will not see ≥55", my last chance, "No thanks, at left it at
that!"

Part 16
Even when pregnant . . . Not by the bugs
But by 2 legged man and not by a science man
Not nice at all supposed to be a knowledge man
Noticed whose theory were to disturb me . . . reassuring its ok
Discriminating dyslexic I may be . . .
At diner he can explain it to me . . . No thanks, this is not me, bang at that!
Do not want to get your bad bugs, take all your Biochemistry

Part 17
In "94 proofed my theory
An VRE would transfer VANCO gene
As an existing co-infection-
VRE with a staph becomes MRSA . . . As it carries its gene
Sub populations of Enterococcus hiding as "SVS"
As it creeps in now finds a new home an MD in 2009 wants to claim she
writes what I wrote
Who would believe, am only a Med Tech were the claims?

Part 18
I've learned to survived
For I have so much love
Love than very few man has
Where did I get it from?
I got from the Gods
I was born the 1st of the All the Saints, named Goddess of wisdom and
symbol Owl, bang!
I never ask for that . . .

Part 19
I drive a GM Cadillac
I don't react to that . . .
It's grey
Even though my heart is not
I response only to love
I can't stand green but love the environment
I love words for a blank page I can fill . . . I just hate how I got it, but it
comes from God, bang

Part 20
My mentor approved my Mobi thesis . . .
Never knew any of its reasons at all
Where and all the why's this bug bugs as a BV,
She with no knowledge at all,
I entered Fall
Though supposed to hold with high morale's . . .
She carried it all to the trash making me fall

Part 21
Handling this bug
To her Ass . . . istant
Published my work-
With her witches
Were her wishes
Trashing all of me completely . . .
Getting others against me maliciously

Part 22
Published my work w/o my permission . . .
Kicking me in the ass
Bang what is next for me?
Did I react to all of this
And/or did I just relax and crack as holding all back?
No, not my new style! Bang this!

Part 23
There's more to be bang about . . .
Bang, bang, bang is all about
A bad ass of a boss crept in . . .
A lesson she should learn, not to mess ever again, bang
Now another comes again for too nice was I-
"Don't mistake my niceness for stupidity
Today, I can state, with a bang!"

Part 24
Denting my door knob as broke in . . . Dame you who've sponsored you?
Dirty u!
Displacing all my files
Deleting my documents
Disrupting my PT entry
Deliberately falsely accusing vindictively for didn't liked me,
"Do it all again" tossing all of me, being mean with extremes
Director of the Microbiology of Lab today, I had to fly high with invisible
wings . . . bang

Part 25
I will not cry—
I already done that
Wanting to discrete me, now I can say . . . bang to all that!
Very dirty hands they all have
There have been others . . . who care, are they anywhere?
I am here all that matters for the Gods who will judge . . . I like to end with a
super bang . . .
Am very happy to be alive, know that to all those who tried to hurt all of
me—bang that

Part 26
Who was I?
A cheerleader, a basketball player, track runner, fashion show model, an
honor guard
Eucharistic Minister, a Lector, An activist, Campaigner, an eager leader . . .
To be exact—of the student government
Secretary and Vice President
A NYC marathoner

Part 27
An awardee of such:
Perfect attendance, Service awards, Athletic,
NYC Chancellor Honor Service Citation,
Oral/Written Honor Spanish & Portuguese,
Volunteer, Anaerobic Bacteriology
Merit Scholarship, Citizen Award
Community Service and many more . . . .

Part 28
Recalling my persistence:
12 yrs old a Candy Stripper
Knew how to sew
Cooked with on my own
15 yrs old college entry
A Medical Assistant
A phlebotomist

Part 29
Bang . . .
Bang . . .
Bang
Once again bang that, I survived you can too . . . Remember that!
Bang
Bang
Bang . . . bang, bang dear ones, not dame, well I've survived—bang that

Part 30
Bang once
Bang twice
I can move my hips
I can think . . . I can say I don't care
I can curse but prefer not . . . for I know don't need to, since grown strong . . .
It's not a song but just a talk of Bang, Bang Bang lyrics to me
I can feel the music in me making me all free . . . feel this breeze, I am finally
free

To those I've no longer sharing this great Earth with me.... that I've loved you so very much being: Aracelis Abreu-Leung, Seferino Frias (my dad), brothers: Jose Eliseo, Aureliano and Nicky Frias, Rowena Garcia (sister-in-law), Juan Nunez, Carmen Garcia (mother-in-law), Wilson Garcia, Herbie Webster and others... these written lines I described a lot for you as you've allowed me to experience many parts of you as I write creatively fallen as rains captured. I thank you for all these gifts. I meant it from my heart.

To my wonderful angelic brother-in-law, Wilson Garcia, may you know "You're always in my prayers and I dedicate this book to you along with husband Jose and son James." Know that you have a beautiful heart, a precious mind and unique being you are... We love you.

To the incredible staff at Long Island University, while I pursued my master's degree in Medical Microbiology including Dr. Joseph Morin, Dr. Don Kwon, Dr. Fatama Abo, Dr. Mrinal Bhattacharjee. My colleagues at Jacobi Medical Center including Dr. Stephen Apelroth, Desiree Meighan, Alan Jablonsky, Elaine Hassan, Dr. Carol Harris and NYC Health and Hospital Corporation and future friends at North Well Health.

I like to end with a passionate and constructive advice: "Where ever life takes you, whether is unbelievably great or incredibly tremendous sadness as I have experienced them all. Know you are never alone. No matter how lonely and sad you may feel, know there's always a way out. Get a cat, a dog and/or a doll to find some kind of belongs of love. Pray, seek and you shall find. Promise yourself or your cat that you will live life to the fullest by never, ever...ever giving up!"

I guarantee you... it may seemed you can't hang on. Know there's always the sun that will never betray you as always comes up. There's your chance to start all over again. All your errors and mistakes are erases, as you can once again start all over again... Let no one and no body tell you otherwise. You must be wise and love yourself. You're strong... seek help, which is the strongest of all the things.

Know we can't never give up. If you ever fall, you must get up! As superman may say, you fall to get up. He may be fictional, but is the will of a man that can make you feel like one and indeed you are one. When you wake up every morning and try, you are one...

You may not be him, just think of all the wonderful things to be alive and strive. Know LOVE is powerful. Love heals. Loves forgives. Loves takes away emotional pain. Love an incredible emotion that's all free. Seek it you don't need to be rich. Keep it. Share it.... It's for all human beings to experience, therefore keep it, spray it like the most precious and beautiful unknown flowers. Live harmoniously knowing we have today with the sun. Live, live, live and love this precious life.

Love is the only seed that doesn't require water. Love has no race, doesn't discriminate, and it sounds are musically inclined for all humans to understand. It's a silent language all man understands. Its warmth within sharing of stars. Is a moon to be discover? Discover it today. But know that once you have discovered it keep it. Don't you ever stop... continue your search and carry always with you.

Make it your creed. To all the Women of the World, and Women Day (March 8, 2019), I've become one with you with your suffering, strength and most all will... always continue to shine for this great Earth and your offsprings... whether you've one or not. Accept it either way. Aim always for the greater goods and greatness. Love never ends...Since it's a hidden flower and star, know it's precious. Continue to grow with it, follow that rainbow! Good luck. -Minerva A. Garcia 3/20/19

References

1. In the Microbiology Lab. Published in NYC ASM (American Society Microbiology) and Staten Island Poetry Society and 1199 SEIU News
2. 9/11 Reflections: Minerva Garcia -- Feeling helpless while praying for her brother-in-law. Published Staten Advance Newspaper. August 26, 2011 at 7:57 AM, updated August 26, 2011 at 8:01 AM Poet. http://www.poemhunter.com/minerva-a-garcia/poems/
3. Published 2006. The Supreme, The Words of the Lord, The Journey of A Rainbow- all published International Poetry of American.
4. For Carl Reina II Mom. Published May 17, 2011 Staten Island Advance
5. Ice Cream in the Sun. 1199 SEIU News
6. In the Microbiology Lab. 1199 SEIU News
7. Paper Frog. Staten Island Poetry Society
8. In the Microbiology lab. Staten Island Poetry Society
9. AN AMERICAN SOLDIER. The bridge Newsapaper
10. The Words OF The Lord. Poetry Society of America
11. Read on radio station by **Valerie Smaldone**, the top-rated **DJ** at WLTW-**FM** Light FM. The Love of a Flower.
12. Read on radio station by **Patricia Herrera**, the top-rated **Spanish-DJ** **103.2** Light FM (Suave). El Amor De Una Flor
13. In this book "Surrender to The Moon", Minerva received honors for the following:

Submitted for publication- accepted
Price for Bio cover- won prize
Price front page poetry- won prize

CPSIA information can be obtained
at www.ICGtesting.com
Printed in the USA
BVHW031220020419
544363BV00002B/196/P